THE MIRACLE-STORIES
OF THE GOSPELS

ALAN RICHARDSON
Dean of York

The Miracle-Stories
of the Gospels

SCM PRESS LTD
BLOOMSBURY STREET LONDON

334 01018 7

First published 1941
by SCM Press Ltd
56 Bloomsbury Street, London
Second impression 1942
Third impression 1948
Fourth impression 1952
Fifth impression 1956
Sixth impression 1959
Seventh impression 1963
Eighth impression 1966
Ninth impression 1969
Tenth impression 1972
Eleventh impression 1975

Printed in Great Britain by
Fletcher & Son Ltd, Norwich

DOCTIS INTERPRETIBVS

QVI APVD OMNES GENTES

IN SACRAE SCRIPTVRAE VERITATE

NOSTRO SAECVLO ILLVSTRANDA LABORAVERVNT

HVNC LIBRVM

PACE FLORENTE INTER COLLES NORTHVMBRIANOS INCEPTVM

LONDINII DVM HORRENDI VIOLENTIA BELLI PETITVR CONFECTVM

GRATO ANIMO

DEDICAT AVCTOR

VERBVM DEI VIVVM

VT SAEVITIAM MARIS ITA POPVLORVM INSANIAM COHIBERE POSSE

PACEM MEDIA IN TEMPESTATE REVOCARE

CONFISVS

CONTENTS

THE MIRACLE-STORIES
OF THE GOSPELS

CHAPTER I

THE THEOLOGY BEHIND THE
MIRACLE-STORY TRADITION

1. *The Biblical Designation of God as Power*

THE miracle-stories form an essential and inseparable part of the Gospel tradition, and
their aim, like that of every other part of the tradition,
is to deepen the understanding of the mystery of
Who Jesus is and to set forth the implications of this
recognition for the whole life and conduct of those
who seek to follow Him. They are told against the
background of the theology of the early Church by
preachers and teachers who saw in them not merely
the supernatural ratification of that theology but
rather the means of the instruction of converts in the
truth of it. The miracle-stories formed a characteristic part of the pedagogic technique of the earliest
Christian missionaries. We cannot arrive at a true
understanding of the nature and function of the
miracle-stories in the formation of the Gospel tradition unless we have first seen how they take their due
place in the total theological scheme of those who
first developed and used them as instruments of their
missionary purpose.

I

At the outset we must grasp the fact that the original makers of the Gospel tradition held unanimously the *biblical* view of the nature of God God is for them the personal, active, overruling Lord ; He is the *living* God. Throughout the Bible God is conceived of as *Power*, the original and only Source of Power, from Whom all other manifestations of power in the universe are derivative. There are therefore no limitations to God's power, by which the world was made ; with God all things are possible, and nothing is too hard for the Lord (cf. Mark x. 27, Jer. xxxii. 17, Gen. xviii. 14). Of course, the power of God is not thought of as capricious ; the strong moral sense of the Hebrew people differentiated their view of the power of God from that of the typically " oriental " conceptions ; for the biblical writers God's power is always the expression of His Will, which is *holy* and *righteous*. But to those who held such a conception of God as power, the question whether He could work " miracles "—*i.e.* acts which involve some degree of intervention in the course of nature or history— could present no difficulty. For the biblical writers the question whether miracles are possible is settled in advance by their knowledge of God as the living God, the Lord of nature and history. The issue doubtless becomes an urgent one for those who are concerned with making some kind of synthesis between the Hebrew and the Greek views of the divine nature ; but it is necessary for us, in our attempt to understand the Bible view of God, that we should studiously refrain from importing the problem into our reading of the biblical records.

In the Old Testament God's power is manifested

in the two chief *media* of nature and history. On the one hand, God is Lord of nature : out of some original and primitive characterization of God as a nature-deity, the Giver of fertility and the God of the thunder-storm (cf. Ps. xxix.), there slowly emerges the conception of God as the Creator of the whole world, as we find it fully developed in the Second Isaiah. But this perception would not have emerged had not Jahweh, Israel's God, also been known, on the other hand, as the Lord of history. It was out of the recognition that Jahweh was the Controller of all history, and not merely of the history of Israel, that the necessary corollary ensued, that nature, the theatre of history, was likewise subject to the sustaining and directing power of the one God (cf. Jer. xxvii. 5). The defining characteristic of the Hebrew religion was its *historical* reference, which issues inevitably in the prophetic understanding of Jahweh as the Creator and Sustainer of the entire world, operating through His Word, which is at once the expression of His will and the executor of His power.[1] The God of nature is one with the God of history.

It is historically probable that this distinctively biblical recognition of God as the Lord of history took its origin in those stirring events, deeply impressed upon the race-memory of the Hebrews, by which their national existence was determined— the exodus from Egypt and the deliverance at the Red Sea. The biblical religion was not evolved from some idea or theory concerning God's power, but arose through an actual historical manifestation of that power ; in the Old Testament the historically

[1] Cf. W. Grundmann, in Kittel's *Theologisches Wörterbuch*, Band ii. p. 294.

3

decisive event, which became for the Hebrew mind the symbol and type of all God's comings in history, is the Miracle of the Red Sea. In the New Testament the supreme manifestation of the power of God is the historical resurrection of Jesus Christ from the dead. In both cases God acts, as it were, *ab extra*, achieving a deliverance within history, yet from outside history, which men could not accomplish for themselves. Without the Sign of the Red Sea there would have been no Jahweh-religion, no Israel and no Old Testament ; without the Sign of the Empty Tomb there would have been no Christian religion, no Church and no New Testament. The Sign of the Red Sea, like the Passover itself, was for the Hebrews not merely a commemoration of a dead past, something which had happened once for all in history long ago ; it was also the symbol of the hope of Israel : it carried the expectation of the promised " prophet like unto Moses " (Deut. xviii. 15) and of the Messianic deliverance. As the decisive action of God at the Red Sea became for the Hebrews the determinative centre of their national existence, of their Passover worship, and of their psalms and literature, so the action of God in raising Jesus from the dead became the source of the Church's life and the theme of its preaching, its sacraments, hymns and prayers. The Christian Eucharist became the symbol of God's effective working in history for our salvation. That which the Old Testament had foreshadowed in the story of the Chosen People was now fulfilled and realized through them on behalf of the whole human race : " Our Passover also hath been sacrificed, even Christ " (1 Cor. v. 7). In the biblical revelation the power of God is revealed supremely as decisive action for our salvation in the concrete events of history.

2. *The Power of God in the New Testament*

The New Testament emphasizes the characteristic biblical conception of God as power by its constant ascription to Him of δύναμις. The Hebrew mind does not dwell upon the *Being* of God, but rather upon His *Activity* ; God cannot be known to us in His inner being, but only in so far as He reveals Himself to us by His own activity. Δύναμις, which means both latent capability of action and also power in action, represents the Being of God in His dynamic aspect, that is, the only aspect in which we can know Him. God is pure δύνασθαι, and it is only through His δύναμις manifested in its effects, " the things that are made," that we have knowledge of His " everlasting power and divinity " (Rom. i. 19 f.). God is He of Whom alone it may with propriety be said : πάντα δυνατά (Mark x. 27). All δύναμις is derived or delegated from God, its only source. Hence it is possible to use δύναμις as a synonym for God, and so indeed we find it used (as a reverential circumlocution) in Jesus's reply to the high priest : " Ye shall see the Son of Man sitting ἐκ δεξιῶν τῆς δυνάμεως " (Mark xiv. 62, Matt. xxvi. 64 ; cf. Luke xxii. 69 and Acts vii. 55 f.).

Dalman (*The Words of Jesus,* Eng. trans., 1902, pp. 200 f.) says that " the Power " was used as a name for God, and he gives instances of this use in Jewish literature. He urges that in Acts viii. 10, Simon Magus (as ἡ δύναμις τοῦ θεοῦ ἡ καλουμένη μεγάλη) is really called " God," since the words τοῦ θεοῦ are probably explanatory additions on the part of Luke (cf. Luke

5

xxii. 69). In the Gospel of Peter the exclamation on the cross, " My God, my God . . .," becomes ἡ δύναμις μου, ἡ δύναμις μου. Cf. " My Strength," Ps. lix. 17 ; cf. also Ex. xv. 2, Ps. xlvi. 1 and lxxxi. 1.

The New Testament sometimes speaks of δύναμις as the *instrument* of God's activity. This, however, represents a convenience (or perhaps even a necessity) of language rather than a metaphysical conception. It does not imply a doctrine of hypostatized δυνάμεις (such as we find in Philo), that is, divine attributes represented as intermediate beings which are the agents of God's external activity.[1] The miraculous deeds of Christ are explained by reference to the divine δυνάμεις which work in Him (Mark vi. 14) ; His ability to heal is traced to His possession of God's power (Luke v. 17) ; the power of God raised Him from the dead (1 Cor. vi. 14, 2 Cor. xiii. 4); it works also in the Christian soul (Eph. iii. 7). Indeed, all the events in history to which the New Testament bears witness are attributed to the effectual working of the δύναμις of God.

The N.T. uses several other words which are near-synonyms of δύναμις to convey the same general teaching. We find, *e.g.* βία (force, violent power), ἐνέργεια (power in exercise), ἰσχύς (strength, especially physical), κράτος (might, manifested power), and, most important of all, ἐξουσία (primarily, liberty of action, then *authority*, either as delegated power or as unrestrained, arbitrary power) (cf. Grimm-Thayer, *Lexicon*, p. 160). Ἐξουσία represents primarily the absolute and uncontradictable freedom of action which belongs to God as Creator and to no one else (cf. Luke xii. 5, Acts i. 7). In the Gospels the R.V. renders ἐξουσία by "authority," usually in the text, sometimes in the margin, except in

[1] H. Cremer, *Biblico-Theological Lexicon*, E.T., 1886, p. 220.

three instances : Luke xxii. 53 ; John i. 12, x. 18. Luke deliberately associates δύναμις and ἐξουσία where Mark has not done so (Luke iv. 36, ix. 1 ; cf. x. 19 ; cf. also the question asked of Jesus in Mark xi. 28 with that asked of the disciples in Acts iv. 7). It may be said that δύναμις and ἐξουσία represent the same general meaning ; the fact that they may be used more or less interchangeably implies that for the N.T. writers there is no conflict between God's (or Christ's) δύναμις and His ἐξουσία—that His *power* is equalled only by His *right* (cf. H. B. Swete, *Gospel according to St. Mark*, 2nd ed., 1902, at ii. 10, p. 37).

All power comes from and belongs to God. This assertion is maintained in respect of three different realms of existence. (*a*) All political power is derived from and is subject to God. " There is no (political) ἐξουσία but of God, and those that exist are ordained by God " (Rom. xiii. 1 ; cf. 1 Pet. ii. 14). " Thou wouldest have no ἐξουσία against me," says Jesus to Pilate, " except it were given thee from above " (John xix. 11). (*b*) God's power is exercised also in the supernatural realm, since all the supernatural powers derive their authority from Him. Even the powers of destruction receive their authority from God to exist and to destroy ; this view carries political implications of the utmost importance, as the author of the Apocalypse perceives : it is God Who has given to the Beast and the " scorpions " (etc.) the power to hurt the earth (Rev. vi. 8 ; ix. 3, 10, 19 ; xiii. 12) : Anti-Christ himself derives his authority from God (Rev. xiii. 2, 4, 5, 7). The power of God over all supernatural forces is demonstrated by the fact that He has finally and decisively set them under the dominion of the Risen Christ ; there are no δυνάμεις or ἐξουσίαι among the invisible powers,

7

τὰ ἀόρατα, which can henceforth rival the authority
of Christ, just as there are no divinities among the
" gods many and lords many " of paganism which
may rank with Him (cf. Col. i. 16, ii. 18; Eph. i. 21;
1 Cor. viii. 5 ; cf. also Test. xii. Pat. iii. 1–8).[1]
Nor can these ἐξουσίαι—the various ἀρχαί, θρόνοι,
ἄγγελοι, κυριότητες and δυνάμεις—separate Christians
from Christ, because the Creator has set all these
creatures under His power (Rom. viii. 38 f.), any
more than they can lead them to Him.   (c) There
is also another region in which God's authority
reigns, namely, that of the δαίμονες, those super-
human but not celestial beings which also exercise
power over human life. The ambit of the dæmons
does not extend to the region above the ἀήρ. The
power of God over these beings is demonstrated by
the fact that He subjected them to the authority of
the incarnate Christ and through Him to that of the
disciples of Christ themselves.

The idea of God's δύναμις is closely associated with
and is expressed in other characteristic N.T. words
which denote God's dynamic activity in or towards the
world—πνεῦμα, βασιλεία, σοφία, χάρις, δόξα. (1) In
the Synoptic Gospels δύναμις is conjoined with the
Spirit only by Luke (i. 17, 35 ; iv. 14). In Acts the
promised gift of power (i. 8) is associated in its fulfilment
with the giving of the Spirit at Pentecost. Jesus is
described as " anointed with the Holy Ghost and with
δύναμις " (x. 38). In 1 Cor. xii. 10 and 28 f. St. Paul
includes " miracles " (δυνάμεις) among the gifts of the
Spirit (cf. also Gal. iii. 5, and cp. Rom. i. 4, xv. 13 ;
1 Cor. ii. 4 ; Eph. iii. 16 ; Heb. ii. 4). (2) One of the

[1] On this subject see J. B. Lightfoot, *Comm. on Colossians*, 1879, at
i. 16 (pp. 152 ff.) ; also W. Fœrster, art. *Exousia* in Kittel's *Theol.
Wörterbuch*, Band ii. pp. 564 ff.

ways in which God's activity is described as operating in the world is that of His " reign " ($\beta a \sigma \iota \lambda \epsilon i a$). The coming of God's $\beta a \sigma \iota \lambda \epsilon i a$ in the person and work of Jesus Christ is the theme of the Gospel teaching : it is for those who witness it " a tasting of the $\delta \upsilon \nu \acute{a} \mu \epsilon \iota s$ of the Age to Come " (Heb. vi. 5). $\varDelta \acute{\upsilon} \nu a \mu \iota s$ is a characteristic of the $\beta a \sigma \iota \lambda \epsilon i a$ $\tau o \hat{\upsilon}$ $\theta \epsilon o \hat{\upsilon}$ (Mark ix. 1) and the word is conjoined with $\beta a \sigma \iota \lambda \epsilon i a$ in Matt. vi. 13 (R.V. margin only), 1 Cor. iv. 20 and Rev. xii. 10 ; cf. also Rev. xi. 17 : "We give Thee thanks . . . because Thou hast taken Thy great $\delta \acute{\upsilon} \nu a \mu \iota s$ and didst reign ($\acute{\epsilon} \beta a \sigma \acute{\iota} \lambda \epsilon \upsilon \sigma a s$)." The Kingdom of God is, as it were, an irresistible $\delta \acute{\upsilon} \nu a \mu \iota s$ silently at work in the world (cf. R. Otto, *The Kingdom of God and the Son of Man*, E.T., 1938, p. 74, where he is speaking of the " experience of the $\beta a \sigma \iota \lambda \epsilon i a$ as $\delta \acute{\upsilon} \nu a \mu \iota s$ "). (3) In the doxologies of Rev. v. 12 and vii. 12, $\delta \acute{\upsilon} \nu a \mu \iota s$ is associated with $\sigma o \phi i a$ (cf. also Mark vi. 2, Matt. xiii. 54). When we have regard to the part played by Wisdom in the O.T. as the agent of God in creation, we realize the full significance of St. Paul's description of Christ as the $\delta \acute{\upsilon} \nu a \mu \iota s$ and $\sigma o \phi i a$ of God (1 Cor. i. 24). (4) The grace ($\chi \acute{a} \rho \iota s$) of God is associated with $\delta \acute{\upsilon} \nu a \mu \iota s$ in Acts vi. 8, 2 Cor. xii. 9 and Eph. iii. 7. Amongst the $\chi a \rho \acute{\iota} \sigma \mu a \tau a$ of the Spirit $\delta \upsilon \nu \acute{a} \mu \epsilon \iota s$ are included in 1 Cor. xii. 10 and 28 f. The enabling $\delta \acute{\upsilon} \nu a \mu \iota s$ which Christians receive is the gift of the grace of God. (5) According to the distinctive biblical usage which the N.T. carries over from the LXX., God reveals Himself to faith through His $\delta \acute{o} \xi a$. This word assumes various shades of meaning : divine honour, splendour, might and visible brightness (cf. G. Kittel in his *Theol. Wörterbuch*, ii. p. 251). It is frequently used in the later Targums as a periphrasis for God (cf. Burney, *The Aramaic Origin of the Fourth Gospel*, 1922, p. 37). It is associated with the idea of God's $\delta \acute{\upsilon} \nu a \mu \iota s$ in Mark xiii. 26 (=Matt. xxiv. 30, Luke xxi. 27), Matt. vi. 13 (R.V. margin only), Eph. i. 18 f., Col. i. 11 and in the doxologies of Rev. iv. 11, v. 12,

9

vii. 12 and xix. 1. As in the N.T. generally the miracles (δυνάμεις) of Jesus are manifestations of His δύναμις, so for St. John (who never uses either δύναμις or δυνάμεις) they are manifestations of His δόξα : " This beginning of signs did Jesus in Cana of Galilee, and manifested His δόξα " (John ii. 11). In Rom. vi. 4 St. Paul declares that " Christ was raised from the dead through the δόξα of the Father." The δόξα of God is generally attributed to Christ (cf., *e.g.* John i. 14, Heb. xiii. 21, 1 Pet. iv. 11, Rev. v. 12, etc.) ; Christ is the " Lord of glory " (1 Cor. ii. 8, Jas. ii. 1). Thus, we may say that according to N.T. usage πνεῦμα, βασιλεία, σοφία, χάρις and δόξα are all, like δύναμις, agents or modes or expressions or instruments or even results of the dynamic activity of God.

A consideration of the greatest importance for the understanding of the meaning of δύναμις in the New Testament is the idea of the *veiling* of God's power. This conception, derived originally from apocalyptic sources, colours the whole of New Testament theology. St. Paul works out this theme most explicitly in his teaching about the power of God being made perfect in weakness ; it is one of the deepest convictions of his own personal ministry that the power of God has been made known to him in his own physical weakness and spiritual inadequacy (2 Cor. xii. 1–10). We are ready to trust in God's strength only when we become aware of the limitations of our own ; a self-sufficient humanism is the deadly foe of biblical religion. God's power, though known to us in its reality by faith through the resurrection, stands in this present age under the veil of sense and time and the flesh. It is not apparent to our human eyes, but only through faith, just as the secret of Who Jesus is is understood not by flesh and blood but by the revelation of the Father in heaven (Matt. xvi. 17). The whole Marcan conception of the Messianic secret is an attempt to express in the Gospel narrative this fundamental insight of the New Testament theology : Jesus sojourns amongst men as the Incognito. The contrast between the *weakness* of the incarnate Lord and the living power of the Risen Christ is central to the theology of the early Church : " He was crucified through weakness, yet He liveth through the power of God " (2 Cor. xiii. 4). To know Christ crucified is to know by faith the power of God (cf. 1 Cor. i. 24 and context). It is by the weakness of the Christ Who does not come down from the Cross that God's power is made known to the believers. The birth of Christ, " born of a woman, born under the Law " (Gal. iv. 4), and His human life " in the form of a servant " (Phil. ii. 7), as well as His death on the Cross, which appears to be defeat and weakness, are the means of the breaking through of God's victorious power. The ἀσθένεια of Christ is the veil of the δύναμις of God, whereas the apparent proud δύναμις of men is but ἀσθένεια in the sight of God.

A parallel process of thought may be discerned in respect of some of the other New Testament words which are used to express aspects of the dynamic activity of God. There is a certain *hiddenness* about the βασιλεία of God, which is as yet known only by faith, although it is truly present and effectual in its working. It is possible for men to disregard it if they choose. It is only to the disciples that it is given to know the mystery of the βασιλεία of God (Mark iv. 11). " The Kingdom of heaven is like unto leaven, which a woman took and hid . . ." (Matt. xiii. 33 ; cf. also the Treasure Hidden in a Field, Matt. xiii. 44 ; the

Pearl of Great Price, Matt. xiii. 45 f. ; the Seed Growing Secretly, Mark iv. 26–29 ; and the Mustard Seed, Mark iv. 30–32).[1] It is not without significance that Q records, immediately after Jesus's condemnation of the cities which had failed to perceive the *meaning* of His δυνάμεις, the striking *Agalliasis* passage : " I thank Thee, O Father, Lord of heaven and earth, that Thou didst hide these things from the wise and understanding, and didst reveal them unto babes " (Matt. xi. 25, Luke x. 21). St. Paul likewise develops the theme of the true but hidden σοφία of God, which he contrasts with the wisdom of the world : " We speak God's σοφία, hidden in a mystery, which God foreordained before the worlds unto our glory " (1 Cor. ii. 7 ; cf. the whole passage, i. 10–iii. 23). So also he contrasts the πνεῦμα of the world with " the Πνεῦμα which is of God " (ii. 12), which alone can reveal to us τὰ βάθη of God, the things which the " natural man " can never understand, " for they are foolishness unto him " (ii. 10, 14). Similarly, St. Paul knows of a hidden δόξα, made known to the eye of faith through Christ, but concealed from those who have not faith : " had they known it, they would not have crucified the Lord of δόξα " (1 Cor. ii. 8) ; this δόξα is to be revealed when the sufferings of this present time are completed (Rom. viii. 18 ; cf. 1 Pet. v. 1). But it is pre-eminently St. John who develops most fully the idea of the inscrutable δόξα of God which has been made manifest in Jesus Christ.

At a first glance it might seem that St. John had lost sight of the great problem which the other New Testament writers are seeking to understand, the

[1] Cf. R. Otto, *op. cit.* pp. 138–149.

" hiddenness " of the incarnate Christ's real majesty :
His δύναμις, βασιλεία, δόξα and so on. From the
beginning of his Gospel, it would seem, no secrecy
envelops the person of the Master ; from the moment
of His first appearance He is recognized for Who He
is ; the Baptist immediately testifies that He is the
Lamb of God and the Son of God (John i. 29, 34),
and Andrew declares, " We have found the Messiah "
(i. 41). Certainly there is a contrast here with St.
Mark's account of the gradual opening of the eyes of
the disciples, a process which does not reach its climax
until the incident near Cæsarea Philippi (Mark viii.
27 ff.). It is clear that St. John disregards the psychological and chronological aspects of the disciples'
education concerning the person of their Master. He
is telling the story from the viewpoint of one who is
looking back over a long period of years. But there
is no shift of theological emphasis here. Although
the disciples understand from the beginning Who
Jesus is, St. John does not imply that the δόξα of
Jesus, or the mystery of His person, was visible to
" flesh and blood," to those whose eyes had not been
opened by the divine Light. His long, elaborate
account of the miracle of the opening of the eyes of the
Man Born Blind (ix. 1 ff.) enforces the teaching of the
whole of the New Testament that supernatural grace
is required for the understanding of the truth of the
Gospel. The contrast in St. John's Gospel is not
between a former state of blindness in the disciples
themselves and a later state of enlightenment, but
between the disciples who understand and " the
world " which does not. Indeed, one of the main
themes of the Fourth Gospel is this very problem
with which St. Mark and St. Paul have struggled, the

13

hiddenness of the person of Christ, and St. John poses it explicitly in the question of Judas (not Iscariot) : " Lord, how is it that Thou wilt manifest Thyself unto us, and not unto the world ? " (xiv. 22). Here we have the crucial question precisely stated. Nowhere does St. John affirm that *the world* beheld the δόξα of Jesus, for that would be a contradiction of his teaching : " *We* beheld His δόξα " (i. 14) ; " the world knew Him not " (i. 10). " This beginning of signs did Jesus in Cana of Galilee, and manifested His δόξα, and *His disciples* believed on Him " (ii. 11). As in the other Gospels, Jesus's miracles are σημεῖα, which are understood only by those who believe in Him and obey His commandments ; perhaps this is the reason why St. John never calls them δυνάμεις ; it is not as " mighty works " but as *signs* that they are to be received. Thus, Jesus says to the multitude : " Ye seek me, not because ye saw signs, but because ye ate of the loaves, and were filled " (vi. 26). In this attitude St. John is expressing the common point of view of the New Testament as a whole. He teaches clearly that the δόξα is not seen without faith : " Said I not unto thee, that, *if thou believedst,* thou shouldest see the δόξα of God ? " (xi. 40). To this whole question of the teaching of the Fourth Gospel concerning the miracles we must later return ; but it was necessary here to illustrate the common attitude of the New Testament writers by pointing it out in St. John, where it is often misrepresented or overlooked.

In Matthew and Mark the δόξα of Jesus is referred to only in the references to the *Parousia* of the Lord (cf. Mark viii. 38, x. 37, xiii. 26 ; Matt. xvi. 27, xix. 28, xxiv. 30, xxv. 31) ; it is never used of the earthly Jesus.

Luke, on the other hand, twice speaks of the visible divine glory : that seen by the Shepherds on the appearance of the Angel (ii. 9) and that seen by the three disciples at the Transfiguration and which enveloped Moses, Elijah and Jesus (ix. 31 f.). Kittel is thus justified in saying that in the Synoptics the use of the word δόξα in connexion with the earthly Jesus is severely restricted (cf. his *Theol. Wörterbuch*, ii. p. 252). Luke's usage represents a midway position between the silence of Matthew and Mark on the subject and the Johannine "We beheld His δόξα " (i. 14). The Lucan references testify to the divine origin of Christ and are thus in line with John xvii. 5 : " the δόξα which I had with Thee before the world was." (The N.T. contains, as we have noted, several references to the δόξα of the Exalted Christ of the Easter faith.)

Just as for St. Paul, Christ crucified is the δύναμις of God and the σοφία of God (1 Cor. i. 24), so for St. John, Christ crucified is the δόξα of God. But St. John does not separate in his thought the crucifixion from the resurrection, and God's glory is for him manifested in the series of events which make up the passion and resurrection sequence : Jesus's passion is the gateway of His glorification ; He passes through it serene and unmoved, like a king entering into his kingdom. The prayer for δοξασθῆναι extends through chapters xii.–xvii. (cf. xii. 23, 28, xiii. 31, xiv. 13, xvi. 14, xvii. 1, 4 f.). It is because the cross is central to the thought of St. John (as of every other New Testament writer) that the arrival of the hour of the passion (cf. xii. 23) means that the δόξα of the Father is now fully manifested in the earthly life of Christ—" that they might behold my δόξα, which Thou hast given me " (xvii. 24).

15

3. *Christ the Power of God*

It is clear that the New Testament writers regard Christ's power as none other than the power of God; Christ is the power of God in action. St. Paul describes the Gospel (of Christ) as " the power of God unto salvation to every believer " (Rom. i. 16); elsewhere he says that the word (message) of the Cross (of Christ) is the power of God (1 Cor. i. 18), and he goes on to speak of " Christ the power of God " (i. 24). Jesus is thus not a detached power, a strange, magical δύναμις appearing from nowhere, without " cosmic significance," like Simon Magus (Acts viii. 10). St. John expresses this truth in his own characteristic fashion : " The Son of Man can do nothing of Himself, but what He seeth the Father doing : for what things soever He doeth, these the Son also doeth in like manner " (v. 19). It was God Who raised Jesus from the dead by His power (Acts ii. 24, etc. ; 1 Cor. vi. 14), not some peculiar δύναμις inherent in Jesus in His own right. Similarly the acts of Jesus on the earth, especially His miracles, are the works which God has done through Him ; this truth is stated in St. Peter's speech at Pentecost : Jesus of Nazareth was " a man approved of God unto you by δυνάμεις and wonders and signs, which God did by Him " (Acts ii. 22). Again, in St. Peter's speech to the household of Cornelius at Cæsarea the same truth is emphasized : God anointed Jesus " with Holy Spirit and with δύναμις : Who went about doing good, and healing all that were oppressed of the devil, for God was with Him " (Acts x. 38). It is clear that any interpretation of the miracles of Jesus as the casual acts of a wonder-

16

worker of the Hellenistic type is entirely false to the theological standpoint of the New Testament, which sees in the miracles of the Lord a revelation of the power and of the saving purpose of God. We shall hope to show that the miracle-stories do not constitute a secondary *stratum* of the Gospel tradition which is somehow foreign to the *ethos* of the Gospel in its primary sense ; they cannot be understood apart from the teaching of the early Church as a whole, of which they are a characteristic vehicle.

The New Testament teaches that God's power is delegated through Christ to those who believe on Him. This teaching is intended in a deep spiritual sense, as referring to the power which the believer receives through faith in Him (cf. 1 Cor. v. 4 ; 2 Cor. xii. 9 ; Col. i. 11 ; Eph. i. 19, iii. 16, vi. 10 ; 1 Pet. i. 5). It is symbolized in the life of the historical Jesus by the healing (saving) power which flowed from Him : " All the multitude sought to touch Him, for δύναμις came forth from Him and healed them all " (Luke vi. 19 ; cf. Mark v. 28–30). The Christian community thus possesses its share in Christ's power, which is the ground alike of its existence and of its faith, and which saves the believers from sin, death, the dæmons and Satan. The community is itself enabled to work miracles (cf. 1 Cor. xii. 10, 28 ; Gal. iii. 5 ; Heb. ii. 4), though it is implied in 1 Cor. xii. 29 that this power is not granted to all Christians. St. Paul claimed that he himself had worked miracles (Rom. xv. 18 f., 2 Cor. xii. 12), and several are attributed to him and to other Apostles in Acts (ii. 43, iii. 1–10, iv. 30, v. 12–16, vi. 8, viii. 6 ff., ix. 12 f. 33–35, 36–42, xiii.

6–12, xiv. 3, 8–10, xv. 12, xvi. 16–18, xix. 11 f. 13–20, xx. 7–12, xxviii. 3–6, 7–10). Everywhere it is implied that the power to perform miracles does not belong to the community in its own right, but is a delegated power from God (cf. Acts iii. 12). In His earthly life Christ had delegated this power to the Apostles (Mark vi. 7 ; Matt. x. 1, 8 ; Luke ix. 1, x. 19), and it was assumed that after His resurrection He had not withdrawn this power from them (cf. John xiv. 12, Acts i. 8).

It has been necessary thus to treat at some length the theological convictions of those who framed the miracle-stories of the Gospel tradition, because these stories themselves form a part of the presentation of that theology, or of the handing on of the Gospel which it was the primary aim of the Evangelists to impart. The problem of the miraculous cannot be solved, as the Ritschlian movement tried to solve it, by an enquiry which could be described as purely historical. The futility of attempting to discuss the miracle-stories as though they could be detached from their theological background and purpose has been abundantly demonstrated during the last century of New Testament research. Disregard of the biblical theology leads inevitably to the attempt to explain away the power of God as it has been revealed in history : " Is it not for this cause that ye err, that ye know not the Scriptures, nor the δύναμις of God ? " (Mark xii. 24). The time has come to make a fresh effort to view the miracle-stories in relation to the purpose of the New Testament writings as a whole and of the Gospels in particular. They will then be seen to be, not mere " wonder-stories " told to excite a credulous astonish-

18

ment at the extraordinary feats of a semi-legendary
man-God, but an essential part of the Gospel preaching, of which the true purpose was to awaken faith
in the saving revelation of God's power towards
them that believe.

CHAPTER II

THE MODERN APPROACH TO THE PROBLEM OF THE MIRACLES

1. *The Gospel Miracles as Wonder-Stories*

THE history of the development of modern thought upon the subject of the Gospel miracles has often been told,[1] and it is not our purpose to recapitulate it here. We must rather begin our own enquiry, which takes the form of a re-examination of the biblical evidence, after a brief glance into the cul-de-sac which the modern discussion has entered as a result of the pursuit of the Form-Critical method.

For a long time it was widely believed amongst Christian people that the Gospel miracles were best understood as the ratification of the claim of Jesus to possess divine authority. The miracles of Jesus were " evidences " of His supernatural *status*. As a consequence of this view, which has been widely held since the Renaissance, it has been easy to assume that this represents the intention of the Evangelists in giving to the miracle-stories the prominent position which they occupy in the Gospel narrative. Every generation reads back its own unconscious pre-suppositions into the New Testament. But it ought perhaps to have been obvious that this view of the

[1] See, *e.g.* C. J. Wright, *Miracle in History and in Modern Thought*, 1930 ; or A. C. Headlam, *The Miracles of the New Testament*, 1914.

significance of the Gospel miracles as consisting in their *evidential* value could hardly have had the same appeal in the first century as it had in, say, the eighteenth, for the reason that in New Testament times the ability to work miracles was not in itself regarded as a proof of divinity.[1] The earliest Christian communities would not have denied that the " sons of the Pharisees " could on occasion cast out dæmons (cf. Matt. xii. 27, Luke xi. 19), and the implied assumption is that, when they did so, they were not deriving their power from Beelzebub. If it was irrational to believe that Beelzebub would supply Jesus with the means of destroying his own kingdom, it is equally improbable that he would supply it to the Pharisees. The early Christians would not have denied that, for example, Simon Magus or Elymas could work miracles. Such phenomena might, of course, be the work of super-human forces which were evil, and indeed St. Paul affirms the actuality of such miracles in 2 Thess. ii. 9. In an age which knew nothing of the dogma of the fixity of natural law and in which miracle might be encountered any day there would be less temptation to credulity in the matter of the " evidential value " of the miraculous than in the age of deism and of the domination of the concepts of physical science. Jesus Himself, as we shall notice, rejected the appeal to credulity and refused to gives " signs "—to work

[1] At most the miraculous element in the Gospel story could prove only that Jesus was a good man. Cf. *The Gospel of Peter* : " And the scribes and Pharisees and elders were gathered together for they had heard that all the people were murmuring and beating their breasts and saying, If such mighty signs are wrought at His death, consider how righteous a man He is " (J. Rendel Harris, *The Newly Recovered Gospel of St. Peter*, 1893, pp. 48 f.).

THE MIRACLE-STORIES OF THE GOSPELS

miracles as evidences of His supernatural power and authority. For Jesus, and for the New Testament writers in general, the significance of the miracles lies in their character, or quality, or spiritual meaning, rather than in their impressiveness as mere "wonders" (cf. Acts x. 38). The idea that the significance of the Gospel miracles lies in their " evidential value " is a modern rather than an ancient view, since it depends for its effectiveness upon a prior belief in the immutability of the laws of cause and effect. It is probably true to say, however, that even when they used the argument from the evidential value of the miracles in controversy against unbelievers, Christian minds have always been aware that it was not the appeal to the miraculous which was the foundation of their own faith : " That a man possesses a strange power which I cannot understand," says the author of *Ecce Homo*, " is no reason why I should receive his words as divine oracles of truth." [1]

Yet the idea that the purpose of the Gospel miracle-stories is to be found in their supposed evidential value continually recurs in the modern discussion of the subject and precludes any true understanding of the real nature and function of the miracle-stories in the formation of the Gospel tradition. Thus, the exponents of the Form-Critical method fail to penetrate to the true meaning of the miracle-stories in the Gospels because they apparently think that they were told in order to emphasize the superiority of Jesus as a " wonder-worker." Bultmann is specially impressed by the " non-Christian parallels " to the Gospel miracle-stories, and he thinks that " the miracle-stories of the Gospels possess a remarkable

[1] 5th ed., 1892, p. 45.

resemblance to the Hellenistic miracle-narratives ; the latter accordingly throw significant light upon the problem of their origin or at least of their formulation." [1] He recommends us to read O. Weinreich's work on ancient miracles of healing [2] and P. Fiebig's discussion of Jewish miracle-stories of the New Testament period.[3] In his own volume, *Die Geschichte der synoptischen Tradition* (2nd edition, 1931), he summarizes at considerable length the Greek and Jewish material, drawing largely upon the above authorities.[4] He concludes that the Gospel miracle-stories " arise in the same atmosphere as the Jewish and Hellenistic miracle-stories." [5] Their object is simply to represent Jesus as a mighty wonder-worker. The " faith " which Jesus requires of those who ask for healing does not mean " a faithful relation to the preaching of Jesus . . . but trust in the wonder-worker." [6] He concludes that the Evangelists (and their predecessors who formed the oral tradition) were interested in the miracles of Jesus not as demonstrations of the *character* of Jesus but as proofs of His supernatural power. This power is regarded as functioning in an automatic way and is apparently unrelated to any ethical consideration or didactic purpose.[7]

[1] *Die Erforschung der synoptischen Evangelien*, 2nd ed., 1930, Eng. trans. by F. C. Grant in *Form-Criticism*, Willett, Clark & Co., 1934, pp. 36 f.
[2] *Antike Heilungswunder*, 1909.
[3] *Jüdische Wundergeschichten des neutestamentlichen Zeitalters*, 1911.
[4] Pp. 236–241 and 247–253.
[5] P. 246 (*ibid.*).
[6] P. 234 (*ibid.*).
[7] Cf. *Die Geschichte der s. T.* : " Die wunderbaren Taten sind nicht Erweise des Charakters Jesu, sondern seiner messianischen Kraft bzw. seiner göttlichen Macht. In der Regel wird deshalb auch

M. Dibelius takes a similar view of the purpose of the Gospel miracle-stories.[1] He is impressed by their " secular " nature, or what he calls their " breadth," their descriptiveness, their interest in incidental detail, their topical and personal references, and the obvious pleasure which (he says) their narrators took in relating them for their own sake, and not for the sake of any specially moral or religious value inherent in them. Like Bultmann, Dibelius regards the miracle-stories of the Gospels as being closely parallel, not merely in form, but also in content and motive, to the miracle-stories of the contemporary Jewish and Hellenistic world. The very name which he gives to them, namely, " Tales " (*Novellen*), is intended to imply the more literary and worldly character of the miracle-stories and their similarity to contemporary non-Christian wonder-stories. Indeed, Dibelius does not hesitate to say that some of the " tales " had a non-Christian origin, since they move in an atmosphere foreign to the Gospel *ethos*. " Jewish-Christian narrators would make Jesus the hero of well-known legends of prophets or rabbis. Gentile-Christian narrators would hand on stories of gods, saviours and miracle-workers, re-cast as applying to the Christian Saviour." [2] Dibelius is thus led to make a series of propositions

nicht ein Motiv Jesu genannt, etwa sein Mitleid oder die Absicht, den Glauben zu wecken. Den Evangelisten kommt deshalb auch das Problem nicht zum Bewusstsein, dass in dem Verhältnis von Jesu Wundertätigkeit zu seiner Verweigerung eines Zeichens liegt. Die Wunder sind gleichsam etwas von seinem individuellen Wollen Losgelöstes, automatisch Funktionierendes " (p. 234).

[1] Cf. *From Tradition to Gospel*, Eng. trans. by B. Lee Woolf, 1934 .of *Die Formgeschichte des Evangeliums*, 1934, 2nd ed., pp. 70 ff.

[2] P. 100 (*ibid.*)

concerning the Gospel miracle-stories which must be entirely rejected if the view put forward in these pages is adopted. He asserts that, as contrasted with the paradigms (or pronouncement-stories, as Dr. Vincent Taylor has called them [1]), the " tales " are " secular " in motive and origin, being narrated not by the *preachers* but by a special class of " story-tellers." Each " tale " is an end in itself and is told for its own sake. " It is immediately clear that the purpose of such narratives is not edification in the same sense as in the other short stories (*i.e.* the paradigms), and that they were not intended to be introduced into sermons on salvation." [2] Thus, according to Dibelius, the " tales " were designed to attest the superiority of Jesus as a miracle-worker over all other miracle-workers, saviours and demi-gods.

> " By telling such tales, the pre-eminence of the Lord Jesus could be demonstrated and all other rival gods who were worshipped could be driven from the field " (*From Tradition to Gospel*, p. 96). Just as non-Christian cults resorted to such methods, so also did the Christian cult : " Whoever wished to spread the cult of Seraphis told such stories, and thus miracle-stories became instruments of the mission. The New Testament tales are to be understood as stories of this kind, useful in spreading the new cult. . . . Preaching saved men and illustrated its points by paradigms. But the tales, told by the churches, revealed self-convincing power. Both types gained believers in Jesus, ' the Lord.' Hence it was in accordance with his purpose that Mark included both paradigms and tales in his Gospel " (*ibid.*).

---

[1] *The Formation of the Gospel Tradition*, 1933
[2] *A Fresh Approach to the N.T.*, p. 41.

The standpoint of the following pages is in complete opposition to such views, and the reasons why they are unacceptable will be seen to be involved in our consideration of the New Testament theology in the previous chapter. But it is perhaps worth while pointing out here that Bultmann and Dibelius find great difficulty in attempting to maintain the sharp distinction thus conceived between the purpose of the paradigms (as Dibelius styles them : Bultmann's name is " apophthegms ") and that of the miracle-stories. The truth is that, generally speaking, there is no such distinction, and that the miracle-stories, no less than the paradigms, are concerned with preaching and instruction. Both alike are the work of the same body of preachers and teachers, and there is no need to suppose (with Dibelius) that a separate order of " story-tellers " existed in the early Church. There is not the slightest evidence for the existence of such an order, and St. Paul did not say, " He gave some to be story-tellers " ! In these pages the view will be maintained that the object of the miracle-stories, no less than of the paradigms, is to awaken saving faith in the person of Christ as the Word of God. Hence we have no need to attempt rigidly to classify the Gospel stories into " paradigms " and " miracle-stories," and we may freely admit that there is no clear dividing line between the two groups. Bultmann and Dibelius do not agree as to which stories fall into each group, and other writers who follow the Form-Critical method usually add still other classifications of the stories. All of them seem to agree that certain of the more obvious miracle-stories are not to be classed as miracle-stories at all, but as paradigms, *e.g.* the Healing of the Withered

Hand on the Sabbath (Mark iii. 1–6) or the Healing of the Dropsical Man (Luke xiv. 1–6).[1] About the classification of other stories they do not agree amongst themselves.[2] From our point of view we may regard this as a private quarrel amongst the Form-Critics which does not concern us, since it turns upon an *a priori* notion of what a miracle-story ought to be like and a fundamentally mistaken idea about the distinction in purpose and origin between paradigms and miracle-stories.

Moreover, the distinction is not founded upon an examination of the *form* of the stories alone. There is a greater *formal* affinity between, let us say, the story of the Withered Hand (Mark iii. 1–6), unanimously classed as a paradigm, and that of the Leper (Mark i. 40–45), unanimously classed as a miracle-story, than there is between the Withered Hand and such a unanimously recognized paradigm as that of the Tribute Money (Mark. xii. 13–17). The Form-Critics pay more attention to the content of the stories than their own premises warrant. In certain other cases (*e.g.* the Paralytic, Mark ii. 1–12; or the Syrophœnician's Daughter, Mark vii. 24–31) the attempt to classify by *form* breaks down altogether.[3]

All true miracle-stories are held by the Form-Critics to possess a common "form," which consists (according to Bultmann) in a "threefold division of the narrative" : (1) The condition of the patient is

[1] Bultmann, *Geschichte*, p. 223 ; Dibelius, *From Tradition to Gospel*, p. 43 ; V. Taylor, *op. cit.* p. 119.

[2] *E.g.* the Exorcism in the Synagogue (Mark i. 23–27), classed by Bultmann and Taylor as a miracle-story and by Dibelius as one of his ten paradigms " of less pure type."

[3] Bultmann and Dibelius are again in opposite camps with regard to the classification of each of these stories.

described, together with the nature, length and gravity of the complaint, and similar details ; (2) the description of the cure is given and the words or acts of the wonder-worker are recorded ; and finally (3) the effect of the cure is demonstrated by the exclamations of surprise on the part of the admiring bystanders or by the behaviour of the patient. (In the case of the nature miracles a similar general form is observable.) Cf. Bultmann, in *Form-Criticism* (*op. cit.*), pp. 36 ff. ; V. Taylor, *op cit.* pp. 121 ff.

It may indeed be questioned whether the *form* of the miracle-stories has any great importance at all. Is anything proved by the discovery that the Gospel miracle-stories bear the same form as the Jewish and pagan miracle-stories of the ancient world ? The fact is that it is impossible to tell the story of a cure in any other way, unless a conscious and elaborate effort is made to avoid the natural mode of expression. A sufferer from hay-fever who describes how Dr. Brown has cured him by the injection of pollinated serum uses precisely the same " form " as that of the miracle-stories of the Gospels or of all the miracle-stories from Seraphis to Lourdes. The " night-starvation " advertisements also use the same " form." [1] But we cannot therefore conclude that the recommendation of Dr. Brown's injections or of somebody's milk-drink " moves in the same atmosphere " or proceeds from the same motives as the miracle-stories of the Gospels, or of Seraphis, or of Lourdes. The discovery of " form " is not very helpful, and an exaggerated use of it is apt to be misleading.

[1] I owe this instructive reflection to Dr. K. E. Kirk.

2. *The Gospel Miracles and the Motive of Compassion*

The modern attempt to find the significance of the miracle-stories in the element of *wonder*, or in the supremacy of Jesus as a wonder-worker, has culminated in the views of the Form-Critics ; but it has carried us very far from the standpoint of the New Testament itself. Others have attempted to find the significance of the miracle-stories in the element of *compassion* ; they were told, it is said, to illustrate the compassionate character of the Lord. But here again we may detect the underlying assumption that the miracle-stories served a different purpose from that of the rest of the material which made up the Gospel narrative, and that it is necessary to find some special reason to account for their inclusion in the tradition. It is our contention that this assumption is entirely unnecessary. Often it is said that the miracle-stories were designed to illustrate both the power and the compassion of Jesus. Thus, Dr. Vincent Taylor writes :

" The miracles are primarily works of compassion and of power. No doubt the idea that the power revealed is Messianic would come in course of time to be stressed, as we see in the Fourth Gospel (x. 25, 37 f., xiv. 11) ; but the Synoptic tradition antedates this stage." [1]

The last sentence presumably means that there was once a time in the development of the Gospel tradition (represented by the Synoptics themselves) when miracle-stories were told to illustrate the power of Jesus before it had occurred to the tellers of the

[1] *Op. cit.* p. 133.

stories that this power was Messianic. If, however, the view adopted in these pages is accepted, it will be seen that neither the Synoptic Gospels nor the miracle-story tradition itself (in any form that is recoverable by us) can be said to belong to such a period, and that the New Testament gives no hint that there ever was such a period at all. Dr. Taylor seems to wish to strengthen our confidence in the historicity of the miracles by showing that the miracle-stories were not originally told as " proofs of the Messiahship and divine right " of Jesus but as stories illustrative of the compassion and power of the historical Lord.

The same assumption underlies the common view that the Fourth Evangelist adopts a different attitude towards the miracles of Jesus from that of the Synoptists. He does not call them δυνάμεις but σημεῖα ; occasionally he uses the relatively colourless word " works " (ἔργα), although it is necessary to add that both " signs " and " works " in the Johannine usage include more than the miracles. It is often stated that the Synoptists do not perceive in the miracles of the Lord the same high significance as does St. John, namely, their significance as *signs*. Thus, for instance, Dr. R. H. Strachan describes what he calls the first main point of difference between the Synoptists and St. John :

" In the case of the Synoptic miracles, we receive the impression that Jesus was always unwilling to work miracles as mere displays, and that when He did heal a man, or miraculously feed a multitude, or still a storm, it was because He was actuated by compassion, or by a desire to help in a difficult or dangerous situation. He exercised His power because He loved men, and in a sense could not help it. In other words, the Synoptic miracles appear to be spontaneous. The motive of compassion, or the character of spontaneity, is not entirely absent in the Fourth Gospel. Prevailingly, however, in the mind of this Evangelist, miracles are *evidential*—evidences or signs that demonstrate Who Jesus is." [1]

As against this view, we would draw no such clear distinction between the Synoptists and St. John. In all the Gospels Jesus is unwilling to work miracles as mere displays, but the motive of compassion is not prominent and certainly is not primary either in the Synoptists or in St. John ; in the Synoptists no less than in St. John the miracles are evidence (not to the general public, but only to those who have eyes to see) as to Who Jesus is. This, we shall maintain, is their *raison d'être* in all four Gospels.

It is true that St. John never mentions the *compassion* of Jesus, and indeed he almost seems to go out of his way to deny that the motive of Jesus in working His miracles is compassion (cf. ix. 3, xi. 4, 15, 42). Yet with that strange paradoxical sense which is so character-istic of the Fourth Gospel, he does call attention to the compassion of the Lord : " Jesus wept " (xi. 35). Even if this latter verse (as many commentators suppose) is intended to indicate Jesus's sorrow over the blindness of the human race as a whole rather than His immediate sympathy for Lazarus and his family, nevertheless in the context in which we find the words it is impossible to escape the conviction that Jesus is touched by the sense of the tragedy of human life and death, so poign-antly suggested by the Evangelist in the Lazarus story.

The truth would seem to be that the Synoptists

[1] *The Fourth Gospel*, 1917 ; Dr. Strachan qualifies this distinction between the Synoptists and St. John later in his book (cf. pp. 75 f.).

and St. John alike present the miracles of Jesus neither as motived nor as unmotived. They are not interested in the question of the motives of Jesus, about which they maintain a consistent and reverent silence. They are not interested in our modern discussion of what is sometimes crudely called " the psychology of Jesus." Occasionally the Synoptists refer to the compassion of the Lord, but more frequently they omit all reference to it, and it is certain that they do not tell the miracle-stories in order to illustrate the motives and attitudes of the Lord. We cannot, we dare not, deny that a motive behind the mighty works of Jesus was compassion, or that they are to be understood as parables of the gracious mercy of God towards those who are in affliction ; we prefer rather, like the Gospel-writers themselves, to exercise a reverent reticence in speaking upon such a subject ; but what we must say emphatically is that the Evangelists do not relate the miracle-stories primarily in order to illustrate the compassion of Jesus. They lived in an age unaffected by the humanistic approach and the humanitarian attitude which are the results of the rise of European liberalism, itself doubtless on its ethical side a product of the Christian conscience which the Church has bred within western civilization. The compassion of Jesus is a subject which has not been foreign to the ethical exhortations of the Church down the ages, though it is never directly mentioned by name in the New Testament outside the Synoptic Gospels ; but it was hardly an argument which could be effectively used by Christian preachers and apologists in an age in which humanitarian emotion was counted as a weakness rather than as a virtue. If we examine the miracle-stories of the Gospels, we find few references to the compassion of Jesus, and we do not receive the impression that those stories have been included in the tradition because of the Evangelists' interest in the motives of the Lord.

St. Mark employs σπλαγχνίζομαι only three times of Jesus (apart from an oblique reference in ix. 22)—twice in connexion with the feeding miracles (vi. 34 and viii. 2) and once in narrating a healing miracle (i. 41 : the Leper). The latter reference is, however, doubtful, since some important authorities read ὀργισθείς instead of σπλαγχνισθείς—a more difficult reading, and therefore probably to be preferred. Mark can therefore hardly be said to be concerned to emphasize that compassion was the motive of Jesus's miracles. Nor indeed can St. Luke, for he omits all the Marcan references to compassion, though he once in a non-Marcan passage attributes this emotion to Jesus (vii. 13 : the Widow of Nain). (Elsewhere the verb σπλαγχνίζομαι is found in Luke only in the parables of the Good Samaritan and the Prodigal Son : x. 33, xv. 20.) It is St. Matthew who, more than any of the other Evangelists, associates compassion with the healing activity of Jesus. He once introduces the idea into a miracle-story from which it is absent in Mark (Matt. xx. 34 ; cf. Mark x. 52) ; in Matt. xiv. 14 (cf. also ix. 35 f.) the healing work of Jesus is mentioned after the Marcan reference to the compassion of the Lord (Mark vi. 34) where St. Mark has not mentioned any healing activity. The Marcan reference to compassion at viii. 2 is reproduced in Matt. xv. 32. On the other hand, in his parallel to Mark i. 41, St. Matthew mentions neither σπλαγχνισθείς nor ὀργισθείς (Matt. viii. 3), which suggests that he did not read σπλαγχνισθείς since it appears probable that he would have retained it in view of his general usage. Thus, of the Synoptists, St. Matthew alone exhibits a tendency to call attention to the compassion of Jesus, but even here the tendency is not strong. St. John never uses σπλαγχνίζομαι ; indeed, the verb is not found in the N.T. outside the Synoptic Gospels.

3. *The Real Problem of the Miracle-Stories*

During the modern period the problem of the miracles of the Gospels was discussed chiefly in terms of whether they happened or not. It was thought to be almost entirely a question of historical evidence and metaphysical possibility. History was understood as a record of objective facts, and facts were things which happened according to objective " natural laws " ; and therefore the enquiry was conducted along two lines—the examination of the historical evidence and the determination by philosophical enquiry of what is possible.[1] If one decided that the miracles of the Gospels really did happen, then their importance obviously lay in their evidential value.[2] But if one decided that the miracles did not happen, it then became a necessary part of Christian apologetic to explain away the miraculous element in the Gospels and to insist that the essence of Christianity was contained in the truth of its teaching on spiritual and moral questions ; and thus it was hoped to commend the Gospel to a generation which had come to believe that God had revealed a fuller knowledge of His truth through the discoveries of natural science. When this stage had been reached, it merely

[1] Thus, Dr. A. C. Headlam begins his book, *The Miracles of the N.T.*, with a chapter entitled " The Problem of Miracles," in which he says, " Our problem is : Did these events happen ? " (p. 3).

[2] To quote Dr. Headlam again : " The Christian religion is a true revelation of what is divine, and the miracles accompanying it are historical, and testify that it is in its origin not of this world."

remained necessary for the Form-Critics to explain how the miracle-stories had come to occupy such a prominent place in the Gospel narrative by relating them to the " parallel " wonder-stories of the Jewish and pagan environment of the Church during the period of the formation of the Gospel tradition.

And yet a survey of the lengthy discussion of the Gospel miracles throughout the whole of the modern period leaves one with the uneasy feeling that something has been left out. What has been overlooked, in fact, is nothing less than the investigation of what the first makers of the Gospel tradition themselves believed about the miracles, or why they came to include miracle-stories in their setting forth of the Gospel of the Word of God. Why did they think that the miracle-stories were so important ? With what object did they relate them ? This is surely a question which comes before our modern question about whether the miracles really happened. The question which we must try to answer is : Why did the earliest missionaries *preach* the miracle-stories ? To such an extent has this problem been overlooked that it has actually become possible for a modern scholar like Dibelius to deny that the miracle-stories had any connexion with the preaching of the Gospel and to imagine that a special class of " story-tellers " was responsible for the development of the miracle-narratives in the tradition of the Church concerning her Lord. So far have we departed from the biblical standpoint that the miracle-stories have come to be regarded as a sort of detrimental off-shoot to the preaching of the Christian message, like a sucker which must be pruned off the rose-tree before it saps the vitality of the flower-bearing stem. We must

35

retrace our steps and ask whether we cannot reach some more convincing explanation of the prominence which the miracle-stories came to receive in the Gospel tradition than an interest in Jesus as a kind of supreme wonder-worker, or in His motive of compassion. The task of the biblical theologian is to ask, first of all, the reason why the miracle-stories were included in the Gospel as an integral and not an accidental part of it. Not until we have done this can we approach the question : Did the miracles really happen ? Then, curiously enough, when we have answered this primary question, we shall find that the secondary question whether the miracles really happened, has answered itself—but we shall not be able to convince those who have not understood for themselves the reason why the stories of the mighty deeds of Jesus became an original and essential part of the preaching of the Gospel message.

It is perhaps worth while to call attention at this point to the high proportion of the Gospel tradition that is devoted to the subject of miracle. Sometimes the miraculous element of the tradition is spoken of as though it represented a merely negligible fraction of the total. In St. Mark's Gospel some 209 verses out of a total of 666 (to xvi. 8) deal directly or indirectly with miracle (*i.e.* over 31 per cent.). If we omit the Marcan Apocalypse (ch. xiii.) from our calculation, about one-third of the Gospel is concerned with miracle. In the first ten chapters of the Gospel (*i.e.* omitting the whole Passion narrative), 200 out of 425 verses deal directly or indirectly with miracle (*i.e.* about 47 per cent.). The absence of the miraculous element from the Passion story is striking : if we do not reckon xi. 1–7, xiv. 12–16, 18–21 and 30 as instances of special miraculous foreknowledge, we are left with only xi. 12–14 and 20–22 (the Barren Fig-tree), and possibly xv. 33 and 38 as instances of the miraculous, *i.e.* a possible eight verses out of a total of 196 (chh. xi., xii., xiv. and xv.), or about 4 per cent.

CHAPTER III

THE MIRACLES AND THE PROCLAMA-
TION OF THE KINGDOM OF GOD

1. *The Powers of the Age to Come*

IF we examine the utterances attributed to Jesus Himself in the Synoptic Gospels on the subject of His own miracles, we find that He regarded them as evidences of the drawing nigh of the Kingdom of God. This is undoubtedly their significance both in the mind of Jesus and in that of the early Church ; the author of Hebrews speaks of Christians as those who have " tasted . . . the δυνάμεις of the Age to Come " (vi. 5). That the mighty works of Jesus are the miracles of the Kingdom of God is plainly taught in the account of the Beelzebub Controversy, recorded both in Mark (iii. 22–30) and Q (Matt. xii. 25–37, Luke xi. 17–23). According to all three Synoptists an accusation was made to the effect that Jesus cast out dæmons through the power of Beelzebub, the prince of the dæmons, to which Jesus replies that even the power of evil cannot be divided against itself, since every kingdom so divided must inevitably collapse. The Q version significantly adds that Jesus went on to say : " But if I by the finger (Luke, Matt. : " Spirit ") of God cast out dæmons, doubtless the Kingdom of God is come upon you." [1] The miracles of Jesus are significant in

[1] Prof. C. H. Dodd (*The Parables of the Kingdom*, pp. 43 f. footnote) says that the phrase ἔφθασεν ἐφ᾽ ὑμᾶς ἡ βασιλεία τοῦ θεοῦ " expresses in

a way in which the miracles wrought by the " sons of the Pharisees " are not, namely, because they are the miracles of the Kingdom of God. They are emphasized in the Gospel story because of the Church's unshakable conviction that the powers of the New Age were manifested in her Lord. The forces of evil were already being overthrown ; the Strong Man's house was already being despoiled by the Stronger, as the following parable in both Mark and Q makes clear.

St. Matthew's alteration [1] of the Q phrase, " the finger of God," to " the Spirit of God " draws attention to an important aspect of the thought of the early Church on the subject of miracle. The working of miracles was one of the aspects, though not the most important, of the activity of the Holy Spirit. In 1 Cor. xii. 7–11 " gifts of healing " and the " working of miracles " are placed in the middle of the list of the diverse manifestations of the Spirit. In the Acts of the Apostles the working of miracles is closely associated with the power of the Spirit. In Rom. xv. 18 f. St. Paul speaks of the things which he had accomplished through Christ " to make the Gentiles obedient, by word and deed, through mighty

the most vivid and forceful way the fact that the Kingdom of God has actually arrived." In both Hellenistic and modern Greek the verb φθάνειν " is used, especially in the aorist, to denote the fact that a person has actually arrived at his goal." He argues that there is no difference in meaning between ἔφθασεν (ἐφ᾽ ὑμᾶς) ἡ βασιλεία τοῦ θεοῦ and ἤγγικεν ἡ βασιλεία τοῦ θεοῦ, and that we should translate both, " The Kingdom of God has come." (Cf. also Luke x. 9–11, Matt. xii. 28, Luke xi. 20.)

[1] It is generally held that Luke's " finger of God " is more likely to be the original Q expression, because the motive of its alteration in Matthew is the obvious desire to avoid anthropomorphism. But we are suggesting that there is a deep theological motive at work in the choice of the alternative phrase, " the Spirit of God."

signs and wonders, by the power of the Spirit of God." In Heb. ii. 3 f. we read that Christ's message of salvation " was confirmed unto us by them that heard, God bearing witness with them both by signs and wonders, and by manifold powers, and by distributions of the Holy Spirit." There is plentiful evidence that the early preaching of Christianity was accompanied by miraculous powers, and that these powers were believed to be manifestations of the presence in the Church of the Holy Spirit, Whose outpouring was regarded as the sign of the drawing nigh of the " last days " (cf. Acts ii. 17 f., Joel ii. 28 f., Isa. xliv. 3, Ezek. xi. 19, Zech. xii. 10). The early Church's belief in miracle through the power of the Holy Spirit was an expression of her eschatological faith. In this context it is appropriate to recall that St. Luke, at the outset of his account of the ministry of Jesus, records the quotation by Jesus in the synagogue at Nazareth of the prophecy : " The Spirit of the Lord is upon Me, for He hath anointed Me to preach the Gospel to the poor ; He hath sent Me to heal the broken-hearted, to preach deliverance to the captives, and recovering of sight to the blind, to set at liberty them that are bruised, and to preach the acceptable year of the Lord " (Luke iv. 18 f. ; cf. Isa. lxi. 1 f.). The healing ministry of Jesus as well as the preaching of the Kingdom of God is here set forth as the manifestation of the activity of the Spirit, which was to take place at the fulfilment of the time, in the " acceptable year " of the Lord.

Considerable attention has been given to the subject of the Kingdom of God in the N.T. in recent research (see esp. K. L. Schmidt in Kittel's *Theol. Wörterbuch*, i. pp. 562 ff. ; G. Gloege, *Reich Gottes und Kirche im Neuen Testament* ; R. Otto, *The Kingdom of God and the Son of Man* (Eng. trans.), and C. H. Dodd, *The Parables of the Kingdom*, ch. ii.). It seems to be generally agreed that βασιλεία means primarily *kingship* rather than *kingdom*, *reign* rather than *realm* : the *kingly Rule* of God. The secondary idea of the βασιλεία as the community over which this kingly Rule is exercised is found only in relatively few passages, and these are usually late (*e.g.* Matt. xiii. 38, 41, 43 ; but cf. also Mark ix. 47 ; Matt. v. 19, vii. 21 ; Luke vii. 28, xvi. 16). The " kingdom " is not a social organization, or an inner religious experience ; it is something which God gives, not something which men " build " or create. Man is judged by the attitude which he adopts towards the rule of God, since he must either accept or reject it. The βασιλεία is thought of as the invincible yet invisible δύναμις of God as it silently operates in the world. Like all the other expressions (*e.g.* πνεῦμα, σοφία, χάρις, δόξα) which denote the fact of God's powerful activity in the world, βασιλεία is essentially a dynamic, not a static, conception. The working of the δύναμις of God results in the manifestation of His βασιλεία.

The charge which was given by Jesus to His disciples as He sent them forth on their mission is reported four times in the Synoptic Gospels and on each occasion the commission to heal is placed alongside of the commission to preach (Mark vi. 7–13 ; Matt. ix. 35–x. 23 ; Luke ix. 1–6, x. 1–20). St. Mark tells us that when Jesus sent out the Twelve He gave them power over unclean spirits (vi. 7) ; St. Matthew adds that He also gave them power to heal all manner of sickness and disease (x. 1) ; while St. Luke in both his accounts says that Jesus sent them to preach the Kingdom of God and to heal the sick

(ix. 2, 6 ; x. 9). Doubtless these stories had first been told in the oral period of the Gospel tradition to guide and encourage the missionaries of the original Jewish-Christian communities in Palestine, since the precise instructions given to the itinerant preachers (Mark vi. 8) must already have been out of date when St. Mark was written ; thus, we have here some first-hand evidence that from the earliest days the ministry of healing was placed side by side with that of preaching in the missionary labours of the Church. Both the Mark and Q versions illustrate this point ; St. Matthew, in accordance with his usual procedure, has conflated both accounts, while St. Luke has apparently followed the Marcan narrative in his story of the Mission of the Twelve (ix. 1–6), and the Q version in his account of the Mission of the Seventy (x. 1–20) ; he doubtless intends the former story to symbolize the mission of Christianity to the Jews (divided traditionally into twelve tribes) and the latter to symbolize the mission to the Gentiles (divided traditionally into seventy nations). A significant Q saying illustrates the connexion in the theology of the early Church between the preaching of the Kingdom of God and the healing work of the Christian missionaries. In St. Matthew's version this saying runs : " As ye go, preach, saying, The Kingdom of heaven is at hand ($\mathring{\eta}\gamma\gamma\iota\kappa\epsilon\nu$) ; heal the sick, cleanse the lepers, raise the dead, cast out dæmons " (x. 7 f.). In St. Luke's version we read : " Heal the sick that are therein, and say unto them, The Kingdom of God is come nigh unto you ($\mathring{\eta}\gamma\gamma\iota\kappa\epsilon\nu$ $\dot{\epsilon}\phi$' $\dot{\upsilon}\mu\hat{a}\varsigma$) " (x. 9).

Another Q saying of the greatest importance is given in almost identical words by St. Matthew and

St. Luke in Jesus's reply to the question of John the Baptist, " Art thou He that should come, or look we for another ? " He answers : " Go and shew John again those things which ye do hear and see : the blind receive their sight, and the lame walk, the lepers are cleansed, and the deaf hear, the dead are raised up, and the poor have the Gospel preached to them " (Matt. xi. 4 f. ; cf. Luke vii. 22). It is clear that both Evangelists understand Jesus to refer to His actual miracles ; St. Luke awkwardly interpolates a verse (vii. 21) immediately before this saying, recording the performance by Jesus of many healing miracles, in order to make this point quite clear. The actual words of Jesus's reply reflect the language of Isa. lxi. 1 and xxxv. 5 f., and there can be no doubt that they are intended to assert that the Messianic Age of the Isaianic prediction had already arrived. The significance of the miracles of Jesus lies in the fact that they are the miracles of the New Age. The things which many prophets and righteous men had desired to see and hear are now presented to the eyes and ears of Jesus's disciples (Matt. xiii. 16 f., Luke x. 23 f.). The mighty works and the preaching of the Kingdom of God are alike witnesses to the fact that the Age of Promise has dawned, and the eyes and ears of the Apostles are blessed by the perception of the signs of its coming.

Inability to perceive the true significance of His miracles was regarded by Jesus as equivalent to the rejection of His Gospel. Those who do not recognize Who Jesus is are not vouchsafed the privilege of beholding the acts of the Messiah ; they have eyes which do not see, and which are not blessed by the vision of the things which the " prophets and kings "

43

had so long desired. This is probably the meaning of St. Mark's statement that Jesus could do no act of power in " His own country " (vi. 5). It would not have occurred to St. Mark to suppose that Jesus's power was limited by the subjective attitude of unbelief amongst the onlookers ; this is a curiously modern view, based upon an unbiblical psychological theory that Jesus's healing miracles were examples of " faith-cures " (in the modern sense), which cannot be performed when " faith " (*i.e.* a form of " suggestion ") is lacking. St. Mark's own qualification—" save that He laid His hands upon a few sick folk and healed them "—ought to have been sufficient to disprove such a theory. St. Matthew has surely no intention of modifying St. Mark's statement ; he merely makes St. Mark's meaning clearer : " He did not many mighty works there because of their unbelief " (xiii. 58). That is to say, Jesus refuses to show the signs of the Kingdom of God to those who will not understand them, since He does not work miracles for their own sake—either as exhibitions of power or as spontaneous deeds of compassion. The working of miracles is a part of the proclamation of the Kingdom of God, not an end in itself. Similarly, the sin of Chorazin and Bethsaida is spiritual blindness ; they do not accept the preaching of the Kingdom of God or understand the miracles which were its inevitable concomitants, according to the prophetic expectation. " If the mighty works had been done in Tyre and Sidon, which were done in you, they would have repented long ago, sitting in sackcloth and ashes " (Luke x. 13, Matt. xi. 21, Q). Even the heathen, it is implied, would have understood from the preaching the meaning of the mighty works, although they did not know the prophets' teaching, and they would have repented. Can we interpret the remarkable connexion which this Q saying establishes between the miracles and repentance in any other way than by understanding the miracles as the necessary concomitants of the preaching of the Kingdom of God ? The saying does not affirm that Chorazin and Bethsaida did not manifest the appropriate degree of astonishment, or even that they did not believe in Jesus as " wonder-worker," but that they did not *repent*. Because the mighty works of Jesus are the miracles of the Kingdom of God, the appropriate response to them is : " Repent and believe the good news." St. Matthew's editorial introduction to the Q saying brings out the point quite forcibly : " Then began He to upbraid the cities wherein most of His mighty works were done, *because they repented not* " (xi. 20).

2. *The Miracles as the Signs of the Kingdom of God*

It is not a matter for surprise that the preaching of the Kingdom of God should have been met with a demand for " signs." The Jewish apocalyptic tradition had taught that the End would be heralded by certain premonitory signs of a supernatural character. At the beginning of his recorded preaching on the day of Pentecost St. Peter had claimed that the portents predicted by Joel had come to pass (Acts ii. 16–20 ; cf. Joel ii. 28 ff.), and he continued significantly : " Ye men of Israel, hear these words : Jesus of Nazareth, a man approved of God among you by miracles and wonders and signs, which God did by Him in the midst of you . . ." (ii. 22). It was natural that the Pharisees should have asked for " signs " of the

45

coming of the Kingdom of God which Jesus preached, and it is apparent from the above quotation that the early Church considered the miracles of Jesus to be the signs of the New Age. Another important piece of evidence concerning the attitude of the early Church may be deduced from the fact that throughout the New Testament the word " wonders " (τέρατα, not found in the singular) is never used without the word " signs " (σημεῖα) [1] ; it is as though the New Testament writers were unwilling to emphasize the miracles as mere *wonders* (as so many modern critics have supposed that they do), but desire rather to point to their *meaning*, their significance as signs. They are not interested in Jesus as wonder-worker, but as the expected Messiah of God.

Yet the Gospel-writers record that Jesus Himself refused to satisfy the demand of the Pharisees for a " sign from heaven." Both Mark and Q contain this tradition. According to St. Mark, Jesus " sighed deeply in His spirit and said, Why doth this generation seek after a sign ? Verily, I say unto you, There shall no sign be given unto this generation " (Mark viii. 12). The Q version (Matt. xii. 39, Luke xi. 29) says that no sign shall be given to this evil generation, except the sign of the prophet Jonah. From the very earliest days the interpretation of this cryptic sign has been open to conjecture. St. Matthew and St. Luke give different interpretations. St. Luke says that " as Jonah was a sign (perhaps he means a warning, a premonitory sign) to the Ninevites, so shall also the Son of Man be to this generation " (xi. 30). St.

[1] Except once in the quotation from Joel (Acts ii. 19) ; but cf. Acts ii. 22.

Matthew explains the saying by means of an improbable analogy between the three days spent by Jonah in the whale's belly and the three days of Jesus's burial in the tomb (xii. 40). Modern scholars have plausibly suggested that the introduction of Jonah is due to a misreading of " John " (the Baptist) under the influence of the subsequent Q saying about the effect of the preaching of Jonah upon the Ninevites (Matt. xii. 41, Luke xi. 32).[1] However this difficult verse is interpreted, it is plain from the combined testimony of Mark and Q that Jesus refused to give a sign to the unbelieving Pharisees. He even suggests that it was morally reprehensible of them to have asked for a sign (cf. 1 Cor. i. 22).

Yet St. Mark leaves us in no doubt that, although He refused to show a sign to the Pharisees, Jesus nevertheless regarded His miracles as " signs." St. Mark proceeds immediately to record the conversation of Jesus with the disciples about the leaven of the Pharisees and of Herod, which arose out of the incident of the disciples' having forgotten to take bread in the ship (viii. 13–21). At first it appears that Jesus is upbraiding the disciples for their anxiety concerning the lack of bread, but it soon appears that He is reproving their inability to perceive the true " sign "

---

[1] J. M. Creed (*The Gospel according to St. Luke*, p. 163) following J. H. Michael (*J.T.S.*, Jan. 1920, pp. 146 f.) suggests that 'Ιωνᾶ is a very early corruption of 'Ιωάνου : John the Baptist is the only sign vouchsafed to " this generation," just as in Mark xi. 27 f., when challenged concerning His authority, Jesus counters with a question about John's authority. A similar confusion between the two names is illustrated by a comparison of Matt. xvi. 17 with John xxi. 15 (cf. John i. 42), R.V. margin.

which He had given to them in the Feeding of the Multitudes. This is a point upon which St. Mark has touched previously, after the episode of the Walking on the Sea (vi. 52). We shall have to discuss later at greater length the full implication of this passage (see below, ch. v.), but here we must briefly point to the deep symbolic meaning which is involved in the narrative. The true " sign " is the Sign of the Broken Bread, the spiritual significance of which had become dear to the Church for which St. Mark was writing in the Eucharist, itself the weekly memorial or " sign " of the Lord's death and resurrection. St. Matthew had seen pre-figured in the " sign of Jonah " the true sign of the death and resurrection of the Lord ; and St. John, in recording the demand of the Jews for a sign, points likewise to the destruction and raising of the temple of the body of Jesus (ii. 18–22), and later he also connects it with the giving of the Bread of Life (vi. 30–65).

Thus, the attitude of Jesus would seem to have been, on the one hand, the refusal to work wonders to compel belief or to satisfy curiosity, and, on the other hand, the insistence that His miracles were truly signs *to those who had eyes to see.* " Having eyes, see ye not ? " (Mark viii. 18). " Blessed are the eyes which see " (Luke x. 23). In both these sayings it is surely correct to understand a deep spiritual meaning in the use of the word " see." We are here confronted by that pervasive idea of the whole New Testament theology, the idea of the veiling of the δύναμις. The truth would seem to be that the early Church regarded the miracles as it regarded the parables, namely, as revelations or signs to those to

48

whom it was given to know the mystery of the Kingdom of God (Mark iv. 11 f.). To the " outsider " the miracles were mere portents, the acts of one wonder-worker amongst many ; to the believer they were unique—not so much in outward form or action, as in their inner spiritual significance as *Gesta Christi*. It was not supposed that the mighty works of Jesus could of themselves compel belief, or that they were intended by Jesus to do so, amongst those who saw but did not understand : " that seeing they may see and not perceive." As mere wonders they were of no more significance than the miracles wrought by the sons of the Pharisees, and Jesus rejected the temptation to perform them. In order to understand them it was first necessary that one's eyes should be opened to the central mystery of the Gospel, the mystery of the person of the Lord ; then they could be understood as the revelation of the power of God Himself. As we shall see, the implications of the Messianic function of the opening of the blind eyes are not overlooked by the writers of the Four Gospels.

It is probable that in the Q story of the Temptation (Matt. iv. 1–11, Luke iv. 1–13) symbolic reference is made to the rejection by Jesus of the temptation to use His marvellous power as a means of compelling belief through the performance of dazzling wonders. In refusing to cast Himself down from the pinnacle of the Temple, Jesus is rejecting the temptation to use miracles in order to attract attention to Himself or to show " signs " to the multitude whose interest He could not otherwise arouse. Creed says : " Perhaps also the narrative reflects a reaction against crude belief in miracle in the early Church," and he adds that " the temptation and its rejection should be set against the background of stories of flights through the air ascribed to wonder-workers. Cf. *Vercelli Acts of Peter*, xxxii. (of Simon Magus) ; Lucian, *Philopseudes* 40 " (*The Gospel according to St. Luke*, pp. 62 f). Dibelius says that the " first point " of the Temptation Story " is to confirm the fact and the reason why Jesus had not done certain miracles ; no miracle of self-help, no miracle of display like casting Himself down from the Temple " (*From Tradition to Gospel*, pp. 274 f.). It is clear that the Gospels maintain this general standpoint concerning the miracles of Jesus, up to the moment when He refuses to come down from the Cross (Mark xv. 32). This line of interpretation is probably true to the early Church's own understanding of the Temptation Story, although it is not the only line which may be adopted. Others have maintained a view which relates the Temptation Story to the political situation of first-century Judea ; thus, according to this interpretation, the refusal to cast Himself down from the pinnacle of the Temple means that Jesus was unwilling to throw Himself in revolt against the Roman might, in blind trust that God would " bear Him up." Such views, however, ascribe to the early Christian communities a political consciousness which we have no reason to suppose that they possessed, and to turn the story into a discourse upon political philosophy which is foreign to the *ethos* of the primitive Church (cf. S. Liberty, *The Political Relations of Christ's Ministry*).

3. *The Miracles as Prophetic Signs*

From the days of the prophets the method of conveying definite teaching or warning by means of " signs " or symbolic actions was well understood. Isaiah had gone about naked as a sign of the desolation which was to come upon the land (Isa. xx. 2 f.) ; Micah had rolled in the dust (Mic. i. 10) ; Jeremiah had worn a yoke upon his neck as a sign of the coming exile (Jer. xxvii. 2 ff.), and Ezekiel had predicted the reunion of Judah and Ephraim by his symbolic joining together of two sticks (Ezek. xxxvii. 15 ff.). At a more recent date John the Baptist had dressed himself in the traditional likeness of Elijah, the expected Forerunner, in order to impress upon his generation that the Judgment was at hand (or, at least, the Christian tradition maintained that he had done so : cf. Mark i. 6 with 2 Kings i. 8, R.V. margin) ; and he had adopted the symbolic ritual of baptism "unto repentance." The Judean-Christian prophet Agabus bound his own hands and feet with Paul's girdle as a sign of the captivity of St. Paul in Jerusalem (Acts xxi. 10 f.). The Gospels record that Jesus Himself used symbolic actions to illustrate His teaching. He took a child and set him in the midst and took him in His arms (Mark ix. 36 ; cf. also Mark x. 13–16). He instructed His disciples to shake off the dust under their feet for a testimony against the unbelieving cities (Mark vi. 11). He exquisitely symbolized the non-political character of His Messiahship by riding into the Holy City on an ass, thus dramatizing the prophecy of Zech. ix. 9 ; and His symbolic cleansing of the Temple clearly pointed to the fulfilment of the prophecy of Mal. iii. 1–3. At the Last Supper with His disciples Jesus performed symbolical acts which became for the Church the most satisfying expressions of the deepest insights of her faith and the vehicle of the most exalted experiences of her worship. St. John records that on this occasion He further enacted His teaching by taking a towel and washing the disciples' feet (John xiii. 4 ff.).

When we bear in mind the wealth of symbolism

which the biblical background thus presents, it is surely unnecessary to look beyond the Bible itself for an explanation of why the miracle-stories often describe the specific actions of Jesus as He performed His wonderful deeds. The Form-Critics make much of the descriptions of the actions of Jesus, such as extending His hand and touching (Mark i. 41), taking the patient by the hand (Mark i. 31, v. 41), touching the part affected (Mark vii. 33, viii. 23, 25) and so on. They choose to refer to such characteristic actions of Jesus in the miracle-stories by means of such phrases as " the miraculous technique," " the manipulative magic of the thaumaturge," or " the technical skill of the therapy." They suppose that the " technique " is described as a model for the Christian miracle-workers. They ransack the literature of the ancient world in order to find " parallels " to the Gospel miracles, and when they have found Jewish or pagan miracle-stories which concentrate upon the " manipulative technique " of the miracle, they then suppose that the miracle-stories of the Gospels have been fully and finally explained. But they overlook the obvious fact that the Bible is always interested in characteristic actions and gestures, and that each of them imparts to the narrative a peculiar *tone* which is not audible save to the ear which can detect the genuine *biblical* ring. In the world of the Bible, signs and gestures count for a great deal ; men fall down on their faces, they kneel in humility or respect, they beat their breasts, rend their garments, kiss one another, laugh and weep, feast and fast, gird themselves, shake the dust off their feet, lift up their heads and cast down their eyes, shave their heads or wear fringes on their clothes—everything is done with a wealth of symbolic

52

action which is quite foreign to the mind of the sophisticated European or American of the twentieth century. It would have been strange indeed if the Evangelists had recorded the wonderful works of Jesus without remarking upon His characteristic gestures, so full of meaning to those who have eyes to see.

And yet there are miracle-stories in the Gospels in which no action of Jesus is recorded and in which it is implied that none occurred. It is the presence of these stories which invites attention and requires explanation, rather than that of those which describe the movements and gestures of the Lord. It is these stories which in themselves are a sufficient refutation of the view that the interest of the stories is centred (as the Form-Critics assert) in the " miraculous technique." For here we are face to face with something that is peculiarly *biblical*. In these stories Jesus heals not with an act, or a touch, or a " medium," but with a *word*. He casts out dæmons with a word (Mark i. 25, v. 8, ix. 25); He calms the storm with His commandment (Mark iv. 39); He cures a blind man (Mark x. 52 ; contrast Mark viii. 22–26) or a withered arm (Mark iii. 5) with His word. St. Matthew stresses the point when he says that " they brought unto Him many demoniacs, and He cast out the spirits *with a word* " (viii. 16). To anyone familiar with the Old Testament it is immediately obvious that the power of Jesus's word demonstrates His participation in the creative power of God, Who both made and rules the world by the word of His mouth (cf. Gen. i. 3, 6, 9, etc. ; Ps. xxxiii. 6, 9, cxlvii. 18, etc.). The significance of the fact that Jesus shares with God the characteristic mode of His creative activity cannot be overstressed.[1] We are moving, not in the atmosphere of Hellenistic magic, but in the wholly opposed thought-world of the Bible. The miracles are included in the Gospel records, not because they are secular tales belonging to the same order as the exorcisms of the Pharisees' sons or the magic of Simon Magus and Elymas, and not because they are better attested or more spectacular or more impressive wonders of this order, but because they are different altogether from these secular wonders ; they belong to a different world-order; they are veritably "the powers of the Age to Come" (Heb. vi. 5), the "signs" of the Messiah, "the works *which none other did*" (John xv. 24).

That Jesus used symbolic actions as the vehicle of His teaching is hardly open to question : that He looked upon His miracles as "prophetic signs" of this nature we can scarcely deny. But to seek to explain away, as some have done, the miracles of the Gospels as being the creation by the later tradition of wonder-stories out of what were originally symbolic acts is to move right outside the atmosphere of the Bible into that of nineteenth-century rationalism. It has been suggested, for example, that the origin of the stories of the feeding miracles was a symbolic act of Jesus, Who blessed the food that was distributed among the multitudes in a sacramental meal, a symbolic "love-feast," in which there was no intention of satisfying the needs of hungry men. Such an

[1] The exclamation of the bystanders after the healing of the Deaf-Mute is highly significant in this connexion : "He hath done all things well : He maketh both the deaf to hear and the dumb to speak" (Mark vii. 37). Christ's work is the "new creation" ; compare this passage, καλῶς πάντα πεποίηκε, with Gen. i. 31 : πάντα ὅσα ἐποίησε, καλὰ λίαν. (Cf. also John i. 3, v. 17, etc.)

54

explanation may, in the case of certain of the miracles, be considered by some to be possible, although it belongs to the realm of subjective interpretation rather than to that of objective historical research ; but in the case of the great majority of the Gospel miracles it is not possible at all. If, for instance, the stories of healings were merely symbolic acts and not positive cures, they would lose their point entirely.

Perhaps the miracle-story in the Gospels which is most obviously suited to this type of interpretation is that of the Cursing of the Barren Fig-tree (Mark xi. 12–14 and 20–25) ; a miracle-story may indeed have been created out of a symbolic act on the part of the Lord, in which, as an Old Testament prophet might have done, He dramatized His teaching concerning the sterility of Pharisaic religion by pronouncing a judgment of doom upon a fig-tree which produced a fine show of leaves but no fruit. A similar judgment of doom is pronounced by the owner of a similar tree in Jesus's parable of the Barren Fig-tree in Luke xiii. 6–9. It may, of course, be that out of a simple parable such as St. Luke here records the later tradition has made a miracle-story. Even those commentators (from St. Augustine to Lagrange) who have regarded the story as true in a literal and historical sense have interpreted it as a symbolical miracle which was enacted as a warning to that class of people about whom Jesus spoke so severely, and who in the Gospels are represented by the Pharisees—the people whose outward religious profession produces no fruits of repentance and good works. Only those commentators who have no understanding of the Christological interpretation of the miracle-stories, that is, of the point of view of the Gospel-makers themselves, can agree with Montefiore in regarding the story of the Cursing of the Barren Fig-tree as possessing " no moral or religious value for us to-day." [1]

The difficulties of regarding the story as literally historical are well known. It was unreasonable to expect to find figs on the tree at Passover-time, as St. Mark himself notices (xi. 13*c*). But the notion of the withering of a fruitless tree is full of symbolical significance and it is to be found in several places in the O.T. As in the Lucan parable, the fig-tree represents Judaism (Luke xiii. 6–9 ; cf. possibly also John i. 48). The leaves of the tree are the empty ceremonies, professions and traditions by which the Jews attempted to cover up the nakedness of their spiritual life—as Adam attempted to conceal his nakedness with fig-leaves (Gen. iii. 7). The fulfilment of the judgments pronounced by the prophets upon such sterile religion is now being accomplished by the Messiah Who " fulfils the prophets " : " I will surely consume them, saith the Lord ; there shall be no grapes on the vine, nor figs on the fig-tree, and the leaf shall fade " (Jer. viii. 13) ; " He hath laid waste my vine, and barked my fig-tree : He hath made it clean bare, and cast it away ; the branches thereof are made white " (Joel i. 7 ; cf. also Ezek. xvii. 24 and Hos. ix. 10, 16 f.). Can we doubt that the earliest Christians saw in Mark xi. 12 ff. a symbolic fulfilment of the prophecies of the Scriptures ? The Marcan context suggests that they did. Menzies (*The Earliest Gospel*, p. 212) remarks that the sayings on faith and prayer appended by St. Mark (xi. 22–26) to the story of the Barren Fig-tree also bear upon the theme of the salvation of Israel. The fate of His own people must

---

[1] C. G. Montefiore, *The Synoptic Gospels*, vol. i. p. 266. He professes to see in this story only " a bad example of what faith can do." Montefiore's treatment of the Synoptic miracle-stories in general may be described as a good example of the pointlessness of reading the Gospels without faith in Christ ; cf. John v. 39 f.

have weighed heavily upon our Lord as He visited Jerusalem at this fateful hour ; the mountain of Jewish unbelief could be removed by God, and Jesus must have believed that what He asked in prayerful faith was being granted, though it was not apparent. The Lucan parable likewise suggests that the tree is to be given another chance (cf. Rom. xi. 26 and the metaphor of the *olive-tree*, Rom. xi. 17–24). Jesus has forgiven His enemies, the Jews (Mark xi. 25, and cf. Luke xxiii. 34).

There can be little doubt that the makers of the Gospel tradition understood the miracles of Jesus as " signs " or symbolical acts which convey in a dramatized form essential Christological teaching. They were enacted parables, not mere " wonder-stories," or occasional works of charity undertaken from motives of compassion in response to a particular and immediate need, or mere historical reminiscences, or yet decorative appendages to the main preaching and teaching material. In the Bible a " sign " is an occurrence, whether natural or supernatural, which authenticates a message or predicts a coming event (cf. Exod. iv. 8 f. 17 ; Isa. vii. 11, 14) ; the signs of Jesus, His miracles, authenticate His message and proclaim the dawning of the Age to Come. But they are signs which are readable only by those who possess the gift of faith ; no sign is given to those who cannot discern " the signs of the times " (Matt. xvi. 3). So, in fact, the historical tradition of the Christian Church from New Testament times has interpreted the miracles of Jesus as the *Gesta Christi*. The classical Christian point of view is well stated by St. Augustine :

" Let us ask of the miracles themselves what they will tell us about Christ ; for if they be but understood, they have a tongue of their own. . . . He was the Word of God ; and all the acts of the Word are themselves words for us ; they are not as pictures, merely to look at and admire, but as letters which we must seek to read and understand." [1]

[1] *In Ev. Joh. tract.* xxiv. ; quoted by Archbishop Trench, *Notes on the Miracles,* p. 291.

CHAPTER IV

THE TEACHING OF THE MIRACLE-STORIES

1. *Jesus as Healer and Bringer of Forgiveness*

WE have seen that the miracle-stories are not to be regarded as a mere decorative appendage to an otherwise complete Gospel tradition ; they form an essential part of the presentation of the Gospel itself. They are in fact instruments or vehicles of the theological or Christological instruction of the early Church, and as such they would be used by the earliest missionaries in their work of preaching and teaching.[1] Many of them contain essential aspects of the original Christian teaching, presented, as it were, in story form. They illustrate the Church's theology and ethics and make them concrete for simple minds ; and they are filled with a profound

---

[1] The words " preaching " and " teaching " are here used in their N.T. connotation. These are defined by Prof. C. H. Dodd (*The Apostolic Preaching*, pp. 3–6) as follows : *preaching* (κηρύσσειν) is " the public proclamation of Christianity to the non-Christian world " ; it is not what we nowadays call preaching. The latter is for the most part *exhortation* (παράκλησις) or *teaching* (διδαχή), rather than preaching in its N.T. sense. *Teaching* (διδάσκειν), in the large majority of the instances of its N.T. usage, is *ethical instruction*. But sometimes it includes what we should call *apologetic*, i.e. " the reasoned commendation of Christianity to persons interested but not yet convinced." " Sometimes, especially in the Johannine writings, it includes the exposition of theological doctrine "—or what we might call instruction in the faith. In this chapter we are using the word " teaching " to cover each of these three senses.

spiritual content which is obscured when they are discussed only from the standpoint of the historian to the exclusion of that of the theologian.

One or two illustrations might make the matter clearer. St. Mark's story of the Leper (i. 40–45) is generally agreed to be a good specimen of the miracle-story " form " ; Dr. Vincent Taylor says that in this story " the form is present to perfection." [1] But to regard it as merely a " wonder-story " designed to illustrate the power of Christ is to miss its deeper meaning. We must approach it in the light of the common biblical assumption that disease is evidence of sinfulness—a belief which is none the less significant for the tellers of the story on account of Jesus's own explicit repudiation of it in its cruder form (cf. Luke xiii. 1–5, John ix. 3). Leprosy was repugnant to the Jew not merely because it was contagious—indeed, an occasional contact with a leper is not a serious matter—the fact is rather that the leper is unclean in a *religious* sense, and he was an outcast not by civil but by religious law.[2] The priests were priests and not medical officers of health. The leper was a sinner, and his life was a living death. We may even suggest that the element of severity in Jesus's attitude towards the leper (represented by the word ὀργισθείς in verse 41, which may well have been the original reading, later altered to σπλαγχνισθείς) may have been intended to represent the divine anger against sin, what St. Paul calls " the wrath of God upon the children of disobedience " (Eph. v. 6, Col. iii. 6). There are sound theological grounds for preferring the more difficult reading in

[1] *Op. cit.* p. 122 ; cf. Dibelius, *From Tradition to Gospel*, p. 71.
[2] Leprosy was regarded as a judgment of God (cf. Num. xii. 9–12).

this verse, but it would perhaps be unwise to over-stress this conjecture, since other explanations are possible.[1] But that other aspect of God's attitude towards the sinner is manifested clearly in the story ; Jesus stretched forth His hand and touched the leper, thereby taking upon Himself the burden of defile-ment. He is revealed by this symbolic action as the sin-bearer. While God's anger towards the sinner is shown in the story—the sinner has no *right* to approach the Holy God, just as the leper ought not to have approached Jesus—He also puts forth His hand to save. Christ enables the sinner to fulfil the demand of the Law, which was formerly his con-demnation ; he may now offer the things which Moses had commanded ; what the sinner could not offer to God through his own merit may now be offered to Him through Christ. The whole Pauline doctrine of justification by faith is expounded in this short *pericope*, which carries us to the very heart of the Gospel message of forgiveness.

Similar teaching is conveyed in the story of the Woman with an Issue (Mark v. 25–34). The woman, who is rendered ceremonially unclean by her affliction (Lev. xv. 19, 25), typifies the sinner who comes to Christ " fearing and trembling," and finds " the δύναμις proceeding from Him " unto salvation. " Thy faith hath saved thee." Others may throng Him, yet know nothing of His gracious power ; only those who, conscious of their own unworthiness, come to Him in faith, are made whole.

The connexion between healing and salvation (in the religious sense) is a characteristic feature of the Gospel tradition. Miracles of healing are, as it

[1] Cf. A. E. J. Rawlinson, *St. Mark*, pp. 20 ff.

were, symbolic demonstrations of God's forgiveness in action. The general biblical assumption that sickness is a consequence of, or even a punishment for, sin underlies the stories of healing and was apparently prevalent in the ancient Church (cf. 1 Cor. xi. 30), despite its criticism in the Book of Job and perhaps even by Jesus Himself (cf. John ix. 3 ; cf. Luke xiii. 1–5). The word μάστιξ (employed of disease in Mark iii. 10, v. 29, 34 and Luke vii. 21) denotes a " scourge," and thus perpetuates the notion that suffering is the punishment of sin. The verb σώζειν is itself ambiguous, meaning, on the one hand, to heal, to rescue from danger, to keep safe and sound, and, on the other hand, to " save " in the technical biblical-religious sense. The same is true of ἰᾶσθαι.[1] The Christian picture of Jesus as the Good Physician, the Saviour of both body and soul, is derived from the miracle-story tradition, which makes use of the healing narratives to convey spiritual teaching concerning salvation. A story recorded by St. Mark culminates in a terse saying of the Lord, which doubtless illustrates the connexion which He Himself perceived between His own healing ministry and His redemptive work : " They that are whole (οἱ ἰσχύοντες) have no need of a physician, but they that are sick : I came not to call the righteous, but sinners " (Mark ii. 17). St. Luke's story of the Sinner-Woman in the house of Simon the Pharisee provides a powerful commentary upon this saying, and it is noteworthy that it concludes with the word of Jesus to the woman, which elsewhere He has spoken after a healing has been performed : " Thy faith hath saved thee "

[1] Cf. J. Weiss, *History of Primitive Christianity*, Eng. trans., ed. F. C. Grant, 1937, vol. i. p. 226 and footnote.

(Luke vii. 50 ; cf. Mark v. 34, the Woman with an Issue).

It should be abundantly clear that the stress upon *faith* in the healing miracles bears small relation to modern psychological examples of faith-healing. The modern use of the word " faith " in the psychological sense has little in common with the faith of which the Gospel-writers are speaking; that is, a saving, personal, believing relationship with Christ. The Gospel miracles of healing are not examples of " faith-cures," and attempts to explain them along these lines are far removed from the spirit of the Gospels.[1] The modern mind which professes to find belief in the healing work of Jesus easier on account of the successes of modern psycho-therapy is still a long way removed from the New Testament faith in Christ the Saviour. The Gospels nowhere suggest that Jesus could not have worked a miracle if the belief that a cure would be effected had been lacking ; they stress the necessity of faith, but it is the faith which illuminates the inner meaning of the miracle, without which Jesus does not consider it to be fitting to accomplish the healing (cf. Mark vi. 5 f.). The Epileptic Boy and Jairus's Daughter are not restored by their own " faith," but because of the potentialities of true Christian faith exhibited by their respective fathers, which gives significance to the acts which Jesus performs (Mark ix. 14–29 and v. 21–43). In each case Jesus speaks to the father concerning faith : " Fear not, only believe " ; " All is possible to him who believes." He is obviously not referring to faith in the sense of auto-suggestion. His reference is rather to that kind of faith of which He said that it

---

[1] Cf. p. 44, *supra*, on Mark vi. 5

" removes mountains " (Mark xi. 23). Jesus speaks of the power of prayer which is offered in faith : " This kind (of dæmon) can come out by nothing, save by prayer " (Mark ix. 29) : " All things whatsoever ye pray and ask for, believe that ye have received them, and ye shall have them " (Mark xi. 24).

Montefiore, who assumes that Jesus speaks of faith in the modern psychological sense, says that Mark ix. 29 is in opposition to the earlier suggestion that it is faith which works the miracle (ix. 23), since it is now stated that prayer works the miracle. But, as we have seen above, no such contradiction is involved, and Montefiore is wrong in his interpretation of the Gospel when he urges that the faith of which Jesus speaks is not faith in the full Christological sense. " It was Paul," says Montefiore, " who first made this faith— faith in Christ as redeemer—the test of salvation. He changed . . . the words ' Follow me ' into ' Believe in me ' " (*The Synoptic Gospels*, i. p. 213). Dibelius likewise asserts that the faith of which the miracle-stories (*e.g.* Jairus's Daughter and the Epileptic Boy) speak is not " the faith which the missionaries preach to the churches, but belief in the power of the miracle-worker. . . . We are not here dealing with saving faith but with the experience of miracle. . . . In the Tales, Jesus is purely and simply the great miracle-worker. . . . Mysterious magic surrounds the figure of the miracle-worker " (*From Tradition to Gospel*, pp. 72–81). Against all such views we insist that the miracle-stories are designed and repeated to convey in story form the theology of the early Church—of the N.T. as a whole, including the Pauline Epistles. The faith of which the miracle-stories speak is the faith which the missionaries preached, and the miracle-stories are themselves part of the preaching. In order to avoid this admission, however, in the interests of his theory of the " storytellers," Dibelius is obliged to class the story of the

Paralytic, to which we must now turn our attention, as a paradigm.

The Christological interest of the miracle-stories is shown clearly in the narrative of the Paralytic (Mark ii. 1–12). To all Jews the power to heal meant the breaking of the power of sin, and this was a function which belonged to the priest (who could *pronounce* whole, even though he had no power to make whole ; cf. Mark i. 44) rather than to the secular medical practitioner. The science of medicine was not looked upon with favour by the more rigorous Jewish leaders, although a more liberally-minded Jew of the Diaspora might agree with Ben Sira that " the Lord created medicines out of the earth, and a prudent man will have no disgust at them." [1] The performance by Jesus of miracles of healing was in itself a scandal to the religious leaders (even when it did not happen on the Sabbath) and it raised the whole question of His person and authority. " Who is this that even forgiveth sins ? " (Luke vii. 49). " By what authority doest Thou these things ? " (Mark xi. 28). So also the high priest's kindred ask a similar question of the Apostles after the Healing of the Lame Man at the Beautiful Gate (Acts iv. 7). The whole discussion of John ix. turns upon the same point : " How can a man that is a sinner do such signs ? " " If this man were not from God, He could do nothing " (verses 16, 33). St. John in this chapter is merely elaborating what is, after all, the dominant interest of the healing-stories throughout the whole of the Gospel tradition,

[1] Ecclus. xxxviii. 4. The whole chapter, though admitting the value of the physician's art, nevertheless maintains the traditional Jewish view that sickness is punishment for sin : " He that sinneth before his Maker, let him fall into the hands of the physician " (verse 15).

the Christological question which they raise (cf. Mark i. 27). The story of the Paralytic raises the question in its acutest form and furnishes us with the most pointed discussion of the connexion between healing and forgiveness. In this story Jesus deliberately implies that His healing work authenticates His power to forgive sins. Whether or not He Himself believed with the Jews that all suffering is punishment for sin (and we have little to guide us on this point), He certainly recognizes here the implication of healing in the matter of forgiveness, as the Jewish mind would have understood it.[1] He accepts the paradox which seems blasphemous to the scribes : only God can forgive sins, yet the reality of the Paralytic's forgiveness is demonstrated by the manner in which he has carried out his bed " before them all." He leaves them with the problem of deciding Who is this " Son of Man " Who thus demonstrates authority on the earth to forgive sins. The importance of this story as part of the teaching material of a Church which claimed in the name of its Lord to be able to forgive sins and to heal the sick (cf. Jas. v. 14 f.) is obvious.

Some scholars—e.g. Wrede, Loisy, Bultmann and Rawlinson (q.v., St. Mark, p. 25)—regard the original of Mark ii. 1–12 as an ordinary miracle-story which told simply of the healing of a paralytic ; vv. 5b–10 are a later expansion due to the theological interests of the community. The sayings later inserted concerning forgiveness have thus the character of the " midrashic " expansions of O.T. narratives, as used for homiletic purposes in the Synagogue. The omission of vv. 5b–10

---

[1] B. W. Bacon (*Studies in Matthew*, p. 391) declares that the connexion between healing and the forgiveness of sin was " inseparable in the teaching both of the Synagogue and of the early Church." Cf. Ps. ciii. 3 : " Who forgiveth all thine iniquities, and healeth all thy diseases."

certainly leaves us with a perfect miracle-story " form " and also removes the difficulty of Jesus's reference to Himself as Son of Man.   Creed, on the other hand, argues that the story as it now stands is a unity, and that the anacoluthon in vv. 10 f. is in keeping with St. Mark's style (*Gospel according to St. Luke*, p. 78 ; cf. C. H. Turner, *J.T.S.*, xxvi. pp. 145 f.).   The real question behind the discussion is whether the question concerning forgiveness is likely to have been debated during Jesus's own ministry, or whether it is one of those questions which would only have become acute during the later controversy between Church and Synagogue. It seems unlikely that the healing activity of Jesus never raised this question at all—assuming, of course, that He really did heal the sick—and we have surely good grounds for thinking that such a question would immediately be asked by the religious leaders.   There is no difficulty in supposing that the conversation recorded in vv. 5*b*–10 is based upon historical reminiscence, and we are under no compulsion to find at all costs a perfect miracle-story " form."   This is one of those cases in which the pursuit of " form " may well be misleading.

It is impossible to over-emphasize the significance of the healing work of Jesus in the subsequent expansion of Christianity throughout the ancient world and indeed in the whole development of Christian civilization.   In a notable essay [1] Harnack has shown how, in a world which had thought of the gods as being interested only in the healthy and strong, the preaching of the Healer-Saviour satisfied a need which the old gods could not meet.   It is significant, he says, that it was Æsculapius, a god of healing, who

---

[1] Excursus ii. appended to his chapter entitled " The Gospel of the Saviour and of Salvation " in his *Expansion of Christianity* (Eng. trans., J. Moffat, 1904), vol. i. pp. 121–151.

held out longest against Christianity. Celsus complained that the latter attracts all the sick and foolish and sinful people ; he had not realized that what the ordinary man needs is not an *explanation* of evil but the defeat of evil. Much has been written about the attitude of Jesus towards the problem of suffering, but we could hardly improve upon Harnack's words on this subject [1] :

> " Jesus says very little about sickness ; He cures it. He does not explain that sickness is health ; He calls it by its proper name, and has compassion upon the sick person. There is nothing sentimental or artificial about Jesus ; He draws no fine distinctions, and utters no sophistries about healthy people being really sick and sick people really healthy. . . . Jesus does not distinguish rigidly between sicknesses of the body and of the soul ; He takes them both as different expressions of one supreme ailment in humanity."

2. *The Authority of Jesus as Exorcist and Teacher*

The Jewish world of the first century A.D. believed firmly in dæmons, and it is hard for us nowadays to realize the extent to which the fear of the dæmons ruled the minds of ordinary folk in those days. The Jews were well known as exorcists of dæmons throughout the ancient world (cf. Acts xix. 13) and amongst themselves the power of exorcism was taken for granted (cf. Matt. xii. 27, Luke xi. 19, Q). Christianity conquered the other religions of the ancient world partly because of its success in casting out the fear of dæmons, and the Christians rapidly ousted the Jewish exorcists from their position of supremacy. The early Church saw in the power of Jesus over the

[1] *Op. cit.* pp. 121 f.

dæmons the earnest of His triumph over Satan, His power to bind the " Strong Man " : " the seventy returned with joy, saying, Lord, even the dæmons are subject unto us in Thy name. And He said unto them, I beheld Satan fallen as lightning from heaven " (Luke x. 17 f.). Or, as St. John puts it in his own fashion : " To this end was the Son of God manifested, that He might destroy the works of the Devil ". (1 John iii. 8). The reputation of Jesus as an exorcist is attested by the fact that, even in His own lifetime on earth, Jewish exorcists had begun to use His name (Mark ix. 38). Harnack, whose essay on this subject is well known,[1] has shown how important in the expansion of the new religion was its success against the dæmons during the first three centuries A.D. In a striking paragraph he sums up the matter thus :

> " It was as exorcizers that Christians went out into the great world, and exorcism formed one very powerful method of their mission and propaganda. It was a question not simply of exorcizing and vanquishing the dæmons that dwelt in individuals, but also of purifying all public life from them. For the age was ruled by the black one and his hordes (Barnabas) ; it ' lieth in the evil one,' κεῖται ἐν πονηρῷ (John). Nor was this mere theory ; it was a most vital conception of existence. The whole world and the circumambient atmosphere were filled with devils ; not merely idolatry, but every phase and form of life was ruled by them. They sat on thrones, they hovered around cradles. The earth was literally a hell, though it continued to be a creation of God. To encounter this hell and all its devils, Christians had command of weapons that were invincible." [2]

[1] Cf. his Excursus on " The Conflict with Dæmons " in *The Expansion of Christianity*, vol. i. pp. 152–180.
[2] *Ibid.* pp. 160 f.

It is not difficult to understand that, against such a background, the power of Jésus over the dæmons would be regarded as a singular authentication of His divine mission and of His teaching : " What is this ? a new teaching ! With ἐξουσία He commands even the unclean spirits, and they obey Him " (Mark i. 27). The relation between the teaching (διδαχή) of the Lord and His authority over the dæmons is strongly displayed in this passage.

The Exorcism in the Synagogue at Capernaum (Mark i. 21–28) is a particularly instructive example of the use to which miracle-stories could be put by the teachers. Dr. Taylor classes it as a miracle-story and Dibelius as a paradigm, but the difficulty of the latter view is that the *pericope* ends not with a " pronouncement " by Jesus but with an exclamation of the onlookers. Rawlinson (*St. Mark*, p. 16) and R. H. Lightfoot (*History and Interpretation*, pp. 68 f.) regard the story as the combination of a general description of our Lord's synagogue-teaching (note the use of the imperfect tense in vv. 21 f.) with the description of a typical case of exorcism. Matthew omits the particular miracle but significantly records the saying concerning how Jesus taught " with authority and not as the scribes " at the conclusion of the Sermon on the Mount (vii. 29). But the teaching of the story *as St. Mark narrates it* is that it is as a result of His possession of ἐξουσία that Jesus both teaches (i. 22) and casts out dæmons (i. 27).

It is interesting, in view of the large part which exorcism plays in the Gospels,[1] to note that St. Paul never refers specifically to exorcism or exorcists in his Epistles, although it is recorded in Acts that he him-

[1] We may notice how frequently exorcism is brought into prominence by the Evangelists in their editorial summaries ; cf. Mark i. 32–34, 39, iii. 11, vi. 7, 13 ; Matt. iv. 24, x. 8 ; Luke vii. 21 (also Acts v. 16, x. 38). See Bultmann, *Geschichte der s. T.*, p. 242.

self exorcized a dæmon (xvi. 16–18). Possibly he includes exorcists in his reference to " workers of miracles " (1 Cor. xii. 10, 29); but he obviously sets no great store upon them either for practical or apologetic purposes.[1] It is altogether improbable, in view of the general belief in dæmons in the Church, that he does not take seriously the existence and reality of the dæmons. He speaks of things sacrificed to idols as " sacrificed to dæmons and not to God " : " I would not that ye should have communion with dæmons : ye cannot drink the cup of the Lord and the cup of dæmons " (1 Cor. x. 20 f.). Harnack drops a hint about why St. Paul passes over the subject of exorcism when he says that " his doctrine of sin was unfavourable to such phenomena." [2] This brings us to an important point. Dæmon-possession was not regarded (as was disease) as a punishment or consequence of sin ; it was just a piece of misfortune which might happen to anyone.[3] The dæmons must inhabit the body of someone—even swine, if the worst came to the worst—or perish, since they had no body of their own (cf. Matt. xii. 43=Luke xi. 24 ; and Mark v. 10, 12) ; and the choice of a victim was quite fortuitous and irrational. Hence the stories of exorcism do not, like the other healing miracles, raise the question of the forgiveness of sins ; for that reason they would be of less interest to the profoundly

[1] As pointed out in ch. i. Paul does take account of the various " principalities and powers," etc. (cf. Eph. vi. 12); but the dæmons must not be confused with these beings, since their ambit does not extend to the upper air.

[2] *Op. cit.* p. 162 footnote.

[3] It was always conveniently possible to suggest that one's opponents were possessed by a devil. Jesus was thus charged (Mark iii. 30 ; Matt. xii. 24 ; John vii. 20, viii. 48 f., x. 20), as also was John the Baptist (Matt. xi. 18).

religious mind of St. Paul. St. John also, who uses the theme of the healing miracles to introduce the question of forgiveness and authority, gives us no story of an exorcism in his Gospel, doubtless for the same reason. The exorcisms, however, do raise the Christological question in another sense, not only because they demonstrate the supernatural power of Christ over the forces of evil (cf. Mark iii. 22–30, Matt. xii. 22 ff., Luke xi. 14 ff.), but also because the possession by the dæmons of superhuman insight enables them to penetrate the mystery, inscrutable to flesh and blood (cf. Matt. xvi. 17), of Who Jesus is. It is a characteristic of the Marcan tradition that the dæmons bear unwilling witness to that very Lordship of Christ which the Church proclaims : " What have we to do with Thee, Thou Jesus of Nazareth ? Art Thou come to destroy us ? I know Thee, Who Thou art, the Holy One of God " (Mark i. 24) ; " What have I to do with Thee, Jesus, Thou Son of the Most High God ? " (Mark v. 7). " He suffered not the dæmons to speak, because they knew Him " (Mark i. 34 ; cf. iii. 11). Thus, even the dæmons play their part in the preaching of the Lordship of Jesus, and the exorcisms supply material for the Evangelists : " the devils also believe and tremble " (Jas. ii. 19).

The story of Legion (Mark v. 1–20) is often fastened upon by modern critics as an example of the " unedifying " character of the miracle-stories, and it therefore demands special attention here. Many scholars agree with Montefiore's view that it was originally a piece of Palestinian folk-magic, a story related of some Jewish exorcist, which has been " fathered upon Jesus " (*The Synoptic Gospels*, vol. i. p. 111). Dibelius says that the tale is full of secular motives, has no teaching value and is foreign to the *ethos* of the Gospel (*From Tradition to Gospel*, pp. 89 ff. and 292). We must, of course, admit that the precise determination of what exactly happened cannot be established. A demoniac was restored by Jesus, and during the course of the exorcism (or shortly afterwards) a herd of swine plunged to destruction in the Sea of Galilee. We may, if we wish, rationalize the story (as some have done) by saying that Jesus cured the poor demented man by offering His friendship and by showing that He was not afraid of him ; that a herd of swine, frightened by the approach of strangers, dashed over a nearby precipice and perished ; and that Jesus quickly pointed the moral concerning the havoc which can be wrought by the " dæmon " of fear. . . . But if we stop here, we shall miss the lesson of the story as it was understood by its original Jewish-Christian narrators. If we put out of our minds all modern humanitarian sentiments about kindness to animals, and remember the fixed ideas of the first-century Jews concerning the dæmons, we shall not imagine that the story is inconsistent with the character of Jesus or devoid of profound spiritual teaching. Dæmons were compelled by the necessity of their existence to incarnate themselves in human or animal bodies, and if they were driven out of one man, they would enter another. Jesus performs a thoroughly " humanitarian " act in allowing them to enter the swine, an act which is not inconsistent with the character of Him Who said : " Ye are of more value than many sparrows." He might have said " swine " ! The story teaches that evil is self-destructive ; it cannot exist by itself, but only in so far as it can gain a foothold in the good. Satan is divided against himself, and his kingdom falls ; the power of God is shown even when the evil forces have their own way. To the Jewish conscience there would be nothing offensive in the idea of the destruction of the swine, which in accordance with the Law (Lev. xi. 7) were regarded as " unclean," and it would be appropriate that the swine should be chosen as the habitation of the dæmons, which are alternatively described as " unclean " and " evil." The fact that we do not share first-century Jewish ideas about dæmon-possession or about " clean " and " unclean " animals should not render us incapable of appreciating the spiritual truths which are embodied in such a miracle-story as this. (It may be noted that it was generally held that a demoniac could be inhabited by more than one dæmon at once : cf. Mark i. 24, xvi. 9 ; Matt. xii. 45, etc.)

3. *Instruction and Exhortation in the Miracle-Stories*

Miracle-stories contain much that is valuable for the Christian teachers ; they stress some aspect of Christian faith or life which is useful in the instruction or exhortation of the Christian community. For instance, the story of Jairus's Daughter (Mark v. 22–24, 35–43), besides containing a lesson on the subject of faith, includes also some important teaching on the Christian attitude towards death. We learn from St. Paul that the fact that some believers had died before the return of the Lord had caused great bewilderment (1 Thess. iv. 13–18) ; some had even been led to deny the resurrection of the dead (1 Cor. xv. 12). The Christian attitude towards death must be taught : death was a sleep (cf. Matt. xxvii. 52 ; John xi. 11–13 ; Acts vii. 60, xiii. 36 ; 1 Cor. vii. 39, xi. 30, xv. 6, 18, 20, 51 ; 1 Thess. iv. 13–15), and after sleep there comes an awakening. There need be no despair because some had died before the Lord had returned ; the wailers must be put outside. Though many will mock at the Christian hope of the resurrection, the Lord will come and bid the dead arise. Only those who believe are admitted to the knowledge of the mystery ; the others are excluded. The Evangelists undoubtedly held that He Who had raised Jairus's Daughter, the Widow's Son and Lazarus would likewise raise all those who had died in Him ; these miracles were but the signs of the greater resurrection which He would accomplish on His return in glory. To raise the dead was a Messianic function, and a Q saying records Jesus's own claim to have raised the dead (Matt. xi. 4 f., Luke vii. 22).

> To seek to rationalize this miracle by suggesting that the words " not dead but sleeping " should be taken quite literally is to misunderstand its meaning and to ignore the N.T. representation of death as a sleep. These words of Christ, which have brought comfort to many mourners, mean : " Not passed for ever out of existence, but awaiting the call of God to the resurrection." Dibelius has again missed the great lesson which this story was intended to teach : he says that it " furnishes no didactic motive," that the Aramaic formula is intended as a magical *recipe* for Christian wonder-workers, and that the admission of the three disciples and the parents only implies an " epiphany " —" the vision of God is not granted to the majority " (*From Tradition to Gospel*, pp. 80 ff.). All this ignores the framework of N.T. theology in which the miracle-stories are embedded in the Gospels. We have suggested above an alternative interpretation of the meaning of the story, which is more in keeping with the N.T. outlook as a whole.

Even such a brief story as that of Simon's Wife's Mother (Mark i. 29–31) contains material for exhortation which we may be sure that the Christian teachers would not be slow to utilize. Here we have, greatly compressed, the perfect " form " of the miracle-

75

story. The sufferer is introduced and her malady is mentioned ; the fact is brought to the notice of Jesus ; the action of the Lord—taking by the hand and raising up—is noted ; the cure is announced, and the proof of its reality is demonstrated by the fact that the fever did not leave the patient exhausted but able to rise up and wait upon her guests. But the story does not merely emphasize the divine power of the Lord ; it contains also a moral exhortation : Christians who have been delivered from the power of sin and restored to health should at once begin to use their blessings in the service of the Lord.[1]

It will be seen that there is not a story which is told of Jesus in the Gospels which cannot be used by the Christian teacher in his work of instruction in the Christian faith and exhortation concerning the Christian life. There is, however, one special problem which confronted the Church's leaders, as well in their ordering of the life and habits of the community as in their ceaseless controversy with the Synagogue, which recurs several times in the miracle-stories—namely, the question of Sabbath observance. It forms the theme of a notable pronouncement-story, the Walking through the Cornfields (Mark ii. 23–28), which concludes with a great saying of the Lord upon this subject : " The Sabbath was made for man, and not man for the Sabbath ; so that the Son of Man is Lord even of the Sabbath." Immediately after this story we find another, in which the discussion of the Christian attitude towards the Sabbath is continued, namely, the Healing of the Withered Hand (iii. 1–6). It is so obviously preposterous to say that this story contains " no didactic

[1] So Trench, *op. cit.* p. 251.

motive " that Dibelius (followed by Dr. Taylor) is led to class it as a paradigm or pronouncement-story. The healing, it is said, is only incidental, and the main " point " is the saying : " Is it lawful on the Sabbath day to do good, or to do harm, to save a life or to kill ? " Yet the *pericope* does not conclude with the saying, but with the miracle, and its effect upon the Pharisees who are provoked to take counsel with the Herodians. The plain fact is that we have here a miracle-story which is something more than what the Form-Critics have decided that a miracle-story ought to be. Its didactic purpose is closely akin to that of the story of the Walking through the Cornfields, and both stories furnish the teachers with material illustrative of the Christian attitude towards Sabbath observance. This motive recurs in several of the stories of healings. Besides the Healing of the Withered Hand there are six other Sabbath-healings (including one exorcism) in the Gospels : The Unclean Spirit in the Synagogue at Capernaum (Mark i. 21–28), Simon's Wife's Mother (Mark i. 29–31—but the fact that the healing in this case took place on the Sabbath is probably an accident of St. Mark's chronological scheme), the Bent Woman (Luke xiii. 10–17), the Dropsical Man (Luke xiv. 1–6), the Impotent Man at Bethesda (John v. 1–18) and the Man Born Blind (John ix). In the Fourth Gospel the question of Jesus's cures on the Sabbath forms an undercurrent of controversy between Jesus and " the Jews " (cf. John vii. 23). The Lucan and Johannine stories are more obviously elaborate literary constructions than the shorter and more direct Marcan stories, but all alike are designed to impart practical instruction on a matter which

77

from the earliest times would seriously perplex the Christian communities.

There are two miracle-stories in the Gospels which contain important teaching of a universalist or missionary character. The first, the Centurion's Servant (Matt. viii. 5–13, Luke vii. 1–10), is, so far as we can tell, the only miracle-story contained in Q.[1] The centurion may well have been one of the " God-fearing " Gentiles. The second story, that of the Syrophœnician Woman (Mark vii. 24–30), is the only other instance of the healing of a Gentile in the Gospels (with the doubtful exception of the Gadarene Demoniac, Mark v. 1–20, who was probably of mixed race). St. Mark obviously desires to stress the fact that she was not a Jew, for he tells us that she was a Greek (*i.e.* by religion) and a Syrophœnician (*i.e.* by race). She was thus a member of an accursed race, doomed by God (Deut. vii. 2). These two stories contain the only examples of cures at a distance in the Gospels (if we count, as we doubtless should, St. John's Nobleman's Son, John iv. 46–53, as a variant of the Centurion's Servant). The fact that they are both healings of Gentiles is surely significant ; the Gentiles, though they have not received Christ in the flesh—a fact which St. Matthew emphasizes by

---

[1] Some critics (*e.g.* F. W. Green, *St. Matthew's Gospel*, p. 157 ; V. Taylor, *op. cit.* p. 75) regard the story as a paradigm and not a miracle-story on the grounds that the real " point " is contained in the pronouncement, " Not in Israel have I found so great faith." Dibelius goes so far as to suggest that in the original Q version there was little narrative, not even a mention of the cure ; Matthew and Luke agree only as far as the pronouncement (Matt. viii. 10, Luke vii. 9). This would mean that Matthew and Luke had made a miracle-story out of a saying. We may add that, if this be so, the process culminates in the Johannine version (the Nobleman's Son, John iv. 46–53), from which the *saying* is entirely omitted !

his interpolated saying, " I was not sent save unto the lost sheep of the house of Israel " (xv. 24)— nevertheless participate through their faith in the benefits which Christ has brought. St. Matthew sees the centurion, as it were proleptically, as the " first-fruits of the Gentiles," the symbol of their ingathering, as he makes plain by his introduction of a saying found in Luke in another context : " Many shall come from the east and from the west, and shall sit down with Abraham and Isaac and Jacob in the Kingdom of God " (Matt. viii. 11, Luke xiii. 29). St. Luke accentuates the idea that the Gentiles do not receive Christ in the flesh by his somewhat elaborate insistence that the Lord did not receive the centurion personally, but only through intermediaries. In the narrative of the Syrophœnician Woman St. Mark gives us the Pauline conception of the divine economy of salvation in story-form : " The power of God unto salvation . . . to the Jew first, but also to the Greek " (Rom. i. 16 ; cf. x. 12) : " Let the children *first* be filled " (Mark vii. 27).

It is sometimes suggested that Jesus's treatment of the woman is harsh. We need to remind ourselves that Jesus does not refer to the Gentiles as " dogs," *i.e.* the pariah dogs of eastern cities, to which the Jews were wont to liken the Gentiles, and which throughout the Bible are a symbol of abomination (cf. Deut. xxiii. 18 ; 1 Sam. xvii. 43, xxiv. 14 ; 2 Sam. iii. 8, ix. 8, xvi. 9 ; 2 Kings viii. 13 ; Job xxx. 1 ; Ps. xxii. 16 ; Prov. xxvi. 11 ; Isa. lxvi. 3 ; Matt. vii. 6 ; Phil. iii. 2 ; 2 Pet. ii. 22 ; Rev. xxii. 15). The word here used by Jesus is the diminutive κυνάριον—a house-dog—not κύων (as in Matt. vii. 6, etc.). No sinister connotation need be read into what is only a harmless and suggestive metaphor.

79

B. W. Bacon aptly entitles this story " The Promise of the Children's Bread to the Gentiles " ; but,
apart from its missionary appeal, it contains another
important piece of teaching, and we might equally
well entitle it, " We ought always to pray and not to
faint." The passage illustrates graphically Jesus's
teaching concerning the necessity of perseverance in
prayer. Those who say that Jesus's reception of the
woman's request was cold and unsympathetic should
ponder upon this aspect of the story in relation to
the whole of our Lord's teaching on the subject
of prayer. He constantly exhorted His followers to
incessant supplication (as distinct from " vain repeti-
tion "), and He Himself wrestled in prayer in
Gethsemane (cf. Luke xi. 5–13, xviii. 1–5 ; cp. Col.
i. 29). The story deals with a perennial problem of
our religious experience. Why did not Jesus accede
immediately to the woman's request ? The answer,
as Archbishop Trench points out, is that blessing is
derived from the struggle itself. He reminds us of
Luther's assertion that the story teaches us " the
method and trick of wrestling with God." It is God
Himself Who enables us to overcome in the struggle ;
it was Jesus Himself Who inspired the faith of the
woman until it was triumphant. The whole theme is
a familiar one to the men of the Bible, who, like Jacob,
have found in God their strength to wrestle with God
(cf. Gen. xxxii. 24–32). " I will not let Thee go,
except Thou bless me."

CHAPTER V

MIRACLE-STORIES AND THE INTER-PRETATION OF THE SCRIPTURES

1. *The Healing of the Blind Eyes and Deaf Ears*

THE Gospel tradition consistently regards the acts of Jesus as the fulfilment of Scriptural prophecy. The Old Testament, it was held, bears unequivocal testimony to the Messiahship of Jesus of Nazareth. The Scriptures thus bear witness to the truth that is in Him. Salvation does not consist, as the Jews supposed, in the Scriptures themselves, but in Him to Whom they bear witness : " Ye search the Scriptures, because ye think that in them ye have eternal life ; and these are they which bear witness of Me " (John v. 39 ; cf. Mark xii. 24, Luke xxiv. 27, Acts iii. 24, etc.). It was not merely that the Church was compelled to engage in controversy with the Synagogue, or that the early preachers had to make their Gospel persuasive to a Jewish audience, but rather that they were themselves Jews, whose whole mind and outlook were saturated in the Jewish Scriptures. The Scriptures formed the text-book for the instruction of their Gentile converts, the prayer-book and hymn-book of their public worship, as well as the source-book for their theology and ethics. Thus, the Old Testament was not a mere interim-revelation, which might be discarded now that the fuller revelation in Christ had been given ; on the contrary, it now became more

important than ever, since the clue to its proper understanding had been vouchsafed. At last, and for the
first time, its true meaning could now be perceived,
for that meaning was discernible only to those who
read in the light of the events of the latter days. Only
those who were in possession of this clue could rightly
apprehend the purport of the Scriptural revelation
(cf. Luke xxiv. 25–27), for the Scriptures are not self-
explanatory and are not to be understood apart from
the interpretation which faith in Christ alone supplies
(Acts viii. 30 f., 35). Given their true Christological
interpretation, they are seen to bear witness to the
truth of Christ, as it was vouchsafed in the Age of
Promise and as it has been fully and finally made
manifest in the Age of Fulfilment. Christ Himself is
thus the Opener of the Scriptures. Hence we find
that in the oldest part of the Church's preaching and
teaching tradition—in the Marcan Passion-story, for
instance, or in the speeches of St. Peter in Acts—as
well as in the later tradition, which culminates in the
Fourth Gospel, an attempt is consistently made to
show forth the witness of the Old Testament to the
Messiahship of Jesus ; and we are not surprised to find
that the makers of the miracle-story tradition were
likewise engaged upon the same task. In this respect,
as in others, the miracle-stories exhibit the same
motives and viewpoints as the rest of the Gospel
tradition.

There are in particular three stories of miracles in
St. Mark's Gospel which call for careful consideration
in this connexion. They are the Healings of the
Deaf-Mute (vii. 31–37), the Blind Man of Bethsaida
(viii. 22–26) and Blind Bartimæus (x. 46–52). Their
significance becomes apparent only against the back-

ground of Old Testament prophecy. According to the writings of the prophets, the opening of the blind eyes and the unstopping of the deaf ears were to be signs of the arrival of the Day of the Lord. The chief relevant passages are :

" In that day the deaf shall hear the words of the book, and the eyes of the blind shall see out of obscurity and out of darkness " (Isa. xxix. 18) ; " And the eyes of them that see shall not be dim, and the ears of them that hear shall hearken. The heart also of the rash shall understand knowledge, and the tongue of the stammerers shall be ready to speak plainly " (Isa. xxxii. 3 f.) ; " Then the eyes of the blind shall be opened, and the ears of the deaf shall be unstopped " (Isa. xxxv. 5) ; " . . . to open the blind eyes . . ." (Isa. xlii. 7 ; cf. also lxi. 1, LXX and R.V. margin, " the opening of the eyes ") ; " In that day shall thy mouth be opened to him that is escaped, and thou shalt speak, and be no more dumb ; so shalt thou be a sign unto them, and they shall know that I am the Lord " (Ezek. xxiv. 27).

It is doubtless because of the way in which the opening of the blind eyes and the unstopping of the deaf ears are conjoined in Old Testament prophecy that St. Matthew places side by side his stories of the healing of Two Blind Men and of the Dumb Demoniac (ix. 27–34), though it seems probable that he has missed the symbolic significance of the Marcan narratives of the Deaf-Mute and the Blind Man of Bethsaida ; perhaps both he and St. Luke felt that the detail of the use by Jesus of the medium of spittle (Mark vii. 33 and viii. 23) and the apparent difficulty experienced by Him in working the miracles were not edifying. But we may be quite certain that it had not occurred to St. Mark to suggest that Jesus experienced

any such difficulty. The " progressive character " of
the story of the healing in Mark viii. 22–26 is due to
St. Mark's desire to symbolize the gradual process of
the unstopping of the disciples' ears and the opening
of their eyes. The story is for him a parable of the
awakening in the disciples' hearts of faith in Jesus's
Messiahship. The Lord reveals Who He is under the
veil of ordinary and vulgar things of sense and flesh.[1]
He leads the deaf man and the blind man " aside
from the multitude " or " out of the village " as He
led His disciples away from the crowds into the desert
or into the neighbourhood of Cæsarea Philippi, where
He was not known and thronged, and there He works
His miracle of imparting sight and hearing. St.
Matthew rightly emphasizes that the revelation near
Cæsarea Philippi was a miracle (xvi. 17), and the New
Testament throughout implies that faith in Christ is a
gift of God.

In order fully to share St. Mark's understanding
of the significance of these two miracles (the Deaf-
Mute and the Blind Man of Bethsaida), it is important
to notice the context in which the Evangelist has set
them. The story of the rejection of Jesus in His own
country (Mark vi. 1–6) marks a turning-point in the
narrative, and we are doubtless intended to see in it
a foreshadowing of the rejection of Jesus by His own
countrymen, the Jews.[2] This, however, does not
hinder the work of preaching and healing, and the
story of the Mission of the Twelve follows immediately
(vi. 6b–13) : if His own kindred will not hear the
message, it must be carried to others. Then comes the

[1] The point is a familiar one in the Fourth Gospel (cf. especially
John ix. 5 f. ; and cf. also Luke xxiv. 30 f. : " He took the bread . . .
and gave it to them. And their eyes were opened ").
[2] Cf. R. H. Lightfoot, *History and Interpretation*, pp. 113, 184 ff.

lengthy section on the death of John the Baptist (vi. 14–29), which acts as the signal for the withdrawal from Galilee and from Herod's jurisdiction. At this point the first of two parallel sections of the Marcan narrative begins. It opens with the Feeding of the Five Thousand (vi. 30–44) and the Walking on the Sea (vi. 45–52), miracles in which the disciples ought to have recognized Who Jesus was, but they did not ; they merely stood " sore amazed in themselves, for they understood not concerning the loaves, but their heart was hardened " (vi. 51 f.). After this the power of the Lord to heal is again stressed (vi. 53–56), the Pharisees' wilful adherence to their own man-made traditions (vii. 1–23) is contrasted with the prayerful faith of the Gentiles (represented by the Syrophœnician Woman, vii. 24–30), and the section concludes with the story of the Deaf-Mute—a Messianic miracle of the utmost significance, which the disciples nevertheless fail to understand. An unconscious testimony to the Lordship of Jesus is, however, implicit in the confession of those who witnessed the result of the miracle : " He hath done all things well : He maketh the deaf to hear and the dumb to speak " (vii. 37).[1] That admission could have only one corollary, but the disciples' hearts are still hardened ; the miracle of the opening of their eyes is as yet only half performed : they see men as trees walking (viii. 24). Jesus now goes back, as it were, and starts the work of opening their eyes over again.

The second of these two parallel sections of St. Mark's Gospel opens, like the first, with a feeding miracle (viii. 1–10), which is again followed by a voyage across the Lake. The narrative of the voyage

---

[1] Cf. supra, p. 54 footnote.

is intertwined with a remarkable passage which emphasizes much more strongly than the first section had done the failure of the disciples to perceive the significance of the feeding miracle (viii. 11–21) : "Have ye your heart hardened ? Having eyes see ye not, and having ears hear ye not ? . . . Do ye not yet understand ? " From this point we pass straight on to the climax, the opening of the eyes of the Blind Man of Bethsaida. Whether the latter was a historical person is a secondary question, though it may be worth while to remark that unless Jesus really healed blind persons, it is difficult to see how the whole elaborate interpretation of the meaning of His sight-imparting miracles could have been built up in so short a time : the important point to notice is that He is certainly a *symbolic* figure. The story represents an enacted parable : the opening of the eyes of St. Peter himself and his companions. The Blind Man of Bethsaida is none other than St. Peter, whose eyes were opened near Cæsarea Philippi. (It is interesting to note that according to John i. 44 St. Peter's home town was Bethsaida.) That this interpretation is no mere fanciful conjecture is demonstrated by the remarkable parallel between the stories of the Blind Man of Bethsaida and St. Peter's Confession, to which Professor R. H. Lightfoot has recently called attention.[1] The latter story (viii. 27–30) follows immediately upon the former, and clause by clause the two are structurally identical, in a manner which we can hardly suppose to be merely accidental. If we compare the two stories (verses 22–26 with verses 27–30), we notice that

[1] *History and Interpretation*, Additional Note B to Lecture III., pp. 90 f.

there is here a definite rhyming of ideas, down to the commands to silence at the end of each.[1] In this way St. Mark has brought out the full Christological significance of the fact that Christ opened the eyes of the blind ; he has shown Him to be, in Johannine language, " the Light of the world," and he has stressed the fact that the possession of saving faith is no mere human achievement but is the gift of God through Christ to helpless men, who blindly grope in the darkness of their unbelief. St. Mark's Gospel thus represents no mere half-way stage in the development of the Christology of the early Church ; we find here not the uncertain struggling towards an adequate apprehension of Christian truth on the part of men who are still tentatively feeling their way, but the mature and confident assertion of faith in Christ as the true source of illumination and understanding. That faith is not obscured by the Marcan symbolism ; on the contrary, an essential part of its content is clearly expressed by it : the *veiling* of the Gospel from those who have not eyes to see or ears to hear. St. Paul gives significant expression to this truth in 2 Cor. iv. 3–6 : " If our Gospel is veiled, it is veiled from them that are perishing, in whom the god of this world hath blinded the minds of the unbelieving, that the light of the Gospel of the glory of Christ, Who is the image of God, should not dawn upon

---

[1] C. H. Turner (*J.T.S.*, xxvi., 1924, p. 18) argues that the correct reading of viii. 26 is not μηδὲ εἰς τὴν κώμην εἰσέλθῃς, but μηδενὶ εἰς τὴν κώμην εἴπῃς, " Tell it to no one in the village." We can see why this reading should have been altered, since it would not have been possible to disguise the effect of the cure ; but St. Mark was not concerned with historical detail but with symbolic interpretation.

them. . . . It is God that said, Light shall shine out of darkness, Who shined in our hearts, to give the light of the knowledge of the glory of God in the face of Jesus Christ." The theology of this passage is the theology of Mark vi. 30–viii. 30.

If our general interpretation of Mark vi. 30–viii. 30 is on sound lines, all theories which attempt to account for the so-called " variants " or " doublets " in this passage by assuming that Mark vi. 45–viii. 26 (St. Luke's " Great Omission ") did not stand in the original draft of St. Mark's Gospel are to be rejected, as Streeter decided on purely literary grounds (*The Four Gospels*, pp. 172–179). We may also dismiss all those theories which seek to explain the actions of Jesus in these two miracles as exhibiting the story-teller's interest in the " technique of mystical magic " (Dibelius, *From Tradition to Gospel*, p. 86), or suggest that the vividness of the stories is due to St. Mark's observance of the way in which Christian healers treated their patients (Rawlinson, *St. Mark*, p. 102), or which attempt to class them amongst non-biblical miracle-stories in which the cure takes place gradually (Bultmann, *Geschichte der s.T.*, p. 138). The explanation of the stories lies in their theological symbolism ; the use of saliva and of the word *Effeta* (a latinization) formed part of the baptismal ceremonial of the Western Church (Rawlinson, *ibid.*), and in one of the early second-century frescoes in the catacombs the healing of a blind man was portrayed among other symbols of baptism (Hoskyns, *The Fourth Gospel*, ii. pp. 402 f.).

The story of Blind Bartimæus (Mark x. 46–52) may be dealt with more briefly. It fits perfectly, as Menzies has noted,[1] into the Marcan " plot " or outline of the life of Jesus. Hitherto only the dæmons,

[1] *The Earliest Gospel*, pp. 202 f.

with their supernatural insight, and the disciples have recognized the Messianic character of Jesus, and they have been forbidden to speak of it ; but now the secret seems to have leaked out, and Bartimæus hails Jesus as " Son of David," in which the Evangelist doubtless sees a reference to the Messianic prophecies of Ezek. xxxiv. 23 f., implying a political conception of the Messiahship. (It may be because of this political connotation attached to the title " Son of David " that Jesus Himself prefers the term " Son of Man " ; cf. Mark xii. 35–37.) The public acknowledgment of His Messiahship is now allowed by Jesus to go unrebuked, and the crowds at the Triumphal Entry likewise take up the cry : " Hosanna ! Blessed is He that cometh in the name of the Lord : blessed is the coming kingdom of our father David : Hosanna in the highest " (Mark xi. 9 f.). Indeed, so far is Jesus from rebuking the acknowledgment of His Messiahship that He now actually endorses it by the performance of the miracle of opening the eyes of Bartimæus. From the standpoint of Christian faith the interpretation of this miracle is obvious : men sit helpless in blindness and poverty until Jesus draws near and they learn to call upon Him. Despite the hindering clamour of the world, they can, if they have faith, hear the voice of Jesus calling to them. When they rise in obedience to His call, they are saved (" made whole ") from their blindness and poverty, and must now begin at once to " follow Jesus in the way " of discipleship. The faith of which this miracle-story speaks, the faith of blind Bartimæus, is not faith in a healer (in the secular sense of " faith-healing ") ; it is rather *Christian* faith, or *saving* faith (verse 52),

89

a faithful relation of dependence upon and obedience towards the person of Christ.

2. Christ as Lord of the Winds and Waves

The significance of the stories of " nature miracles " in St. Mark's Gospel—the two sea miracles and the two feeding miracles [1]—lies in the theological teaching which, as acts of the Messiah, they contain. Like the healing miracles, they can be understood only against the background of the Old Testament, and not in the light of non-biblical wonder-stories. If we wish to understand the meaning of the two sea miracles, we must remember the Old Testament metaphors of the sea, which always remained a sphere of danger, mystery and terror to the Hebrew mind ; the restless sea is treated as the symbol of the troubled and sinful world.[2] The power of Jehovah is supremely demonstrated by His authority over the winds and waves. That Jesus shares the power of God as the Lord of the mysteries of creation is the main teaching of the stories of the Stilling of the Storm (Mark iv. 35–41) and the Walking on the Sea (Mark vi. 45–52). The Christian readers of St. Mark's Gospel already know the answer to the disciples' question : " Who then is this, that even the wind and the sea obey Him ? " (iv. 41) ; and it is suggested that the disciples ought to have understood from the miracle of Jesus's walking on the water Who He was, but their heart

[1] The story of the Barren Fig-tree, usually counted as the fifth nature miracle in St. Mark, has already been discussed (*supra*, pp. 55–57).

[2] Cf. Isa. lvii. 20 : " The wicked are like the troubled sea when it cannot rest, whose waters cast up mire and dirt."

was hardened, and their primary reaction was merely that of amazement (vi. 52).

In the O.T. the majesty of Jehovah as the Lord of nature is frequently stressed by means of the assertion of His power to control the storms and tumults of the sea. The key passage is the great description of the stilling of the storm in Ps. cvii. 23–30 : " They that go down to the sea in ships, that do business in great waters ; these see the works of the Lord and His wonders in the deep. For He commandeth and raiseth the stormy wind, which lifteth up the waves thereof. They mount up to the heaven, they go down again to the depths : their soul is melted because of trouble. They reel to and fro, and stagger like a drunken man, and are at their wits' end. Then they cry unto the Lord in their trouble, and He bringeth them out of their distresses. He maketh the storm a calm, so that the waves thereof are still. Then are they glad because they be quiet ; so He bringeth them unto their desired haven." It is hardly surprising that St. Mark's readers should have seen—as they were intended to see—in the story of the Stilling of the Storm a "fulfilment" of this Psalm. We might also cite : Ps. lxxxix. 9, " Thou rulest the pride of the sea ; when the waves thereof arise, Thou stillest them " ; Ps. xxix. 3, xlvi. 3, xciii. 3 f. ; Nahum i. 4 ; Hab. iii. 15 and Job xxviii. 4 (R.V. margin). St. Mark in iv. 39 implies that Jesus is casting out the dæmon of the storm, since the words ἐπετίμησε ("rebuked") and πεφίμωσο (" Be muzzled ! ") are parallel to the words used in Mark i. 25 (the Exorcism in the Synagogue at Capernaum)—which shows, if evidence were required, that St. Mark recognized no distinction between " healing miracles " and " nature miracles." Hoskyns and Davey (*The Riddle of the New Testament*, pp. 169 and 172) have pointed out that St. Mark may have intentionally placed side by side the stories of the Casting Out of the Dæmon of the Storm and the Casting Out of the Legion of Dæmons (Mark v. 1–20) as an illustration of the fulfilment of Ps. lxv. 7 : " Who stilleth the roaring of the seas, the roaring of their waves, and the madness of the peoples." We have already noticed examples of the way in which St. Mark suggestively places his stories side by side, so that the one will illustrate the other ; another possible example of this practice is the juxtaposition of the Healing of the Paralytic (Mark ii. 1–12) and the Call of Levi (ii. 13–17), with its culminating saying in verse 17, which may well be said to constitute the " point " of both stories.

Besides the primary teaching in the sea miracles concerning the mystery of Who Jesus is, there is a secondary or *paracletic* theme, which brings a message of comfort to a storm-tossed Church in a hostile world, and which would speak a word of special encouragement to St. Mark's first readers, if (as is usually supposed) they were the Christians living in Rome during the days of Nero's persecution. It might seem to the faint-hearted that the Lord was asleep and indifferent to their peril ; but in truth He is present in the Church, and will arise and cast out the dæmon of the storm. Or again, it might seem to the Christians, toiling hard at the oars against the mounting waves and contrary winds of persecution and opposition, that they were making but little headway ; but at the darkest hour of the night (" about the fourth watch," vi. 48, *i.e.* about 3 a.m.) the Lord would come—not as a phantom, but in His full reality, powerful to save— treading on the waves of the storm, and bringing peace, revealing His very Self to those who believe on Him, as Jehovah had revealed His name to Moses : ἐγώ εἰμι (Mark vi. 50 ; cf. Ex. iii. 14, " I AM hath sent me unto you "). The experience of Christ in the

Church is no apparition ; it is the Lord Himself, no subtle self-deception of a wayward imagination ; He brings peace to our hearts in the midst of the storm. If our prayers for His coming do not seem to be answered immediately,[1] the reason is that a tested faith and more diligent perseverance in prayer will become for us the means of a greater blessing.

Such an interpretation of the meaning of the two Marcan sea miracles is, of course, not novel ; it follows the traditional line of the Church's interpretation since ancient times. Out of many possible references we may select a passage from Tertullian (*De Bapt.* 12) as typical of the traditional interpretation : " That little ship presented a figure of the Church, in that she is disquieted in the sea, that is, in the world, by the waves, that is, by persecutions and temptations, the Lord patiently sleeping, as it were, until, roused at last by the prayers of the saints, He checks the world and restores tranquillity to His own." (For many similar citations from the Fathers, see Trench, *Notes on the Miracles*, pp. 152–160 and 295–308.) That St. Mark intended this kind of interpretation to be read into his narratives seems to be beyond all reasonable doubt. In vi. 52 he implies that there is a hidden meaning behind the miracle, which the disciples only later understood in the light of the resurrection. Dibelius is as far as possible from the truth when he speaks of an " epiphany motive " or says that the Walking on the Water is " an example of the secularization of the Christian narrative by non-Christian motives " (*From Tradition to Gospel*, p. 277 ; cf. also p. 100).

---

[1] Cf. Mark vi. 48 : " He would have passed by them "—καὶ ἤθελε παρελθεῖν αὐτούς ; cf. Luke xxiv. 28, " He made as though He would go further " ; and the story of the Syrophœnician Woman, Mark vii. 27 (*supra*, p. 80).

3. *The Making Known of Christ in the Breaking of the Bread*

The two feeding miracles in St. Mark's Gospel—
the Five Thousand (vi. 33–44) and the Four Thousand
(viii. 1–9)—are obviously intended to teach deep
spiritual truth. We have already noticed the significant rôle which they play in the context in which the
Evangelist has set them ; they are acts of the Messiah,
not immediately understood as such by the disciples,
each forming the first stage of the process, twice
attempted, of the opening of the disciples' eyes. The
stories of the feedings, it has often been noticed, do
not conclude with exclamations of amazement on the
part of the bystanders ; which suggests that it was
not in their aspect of " wonder " that St. Mark saw
their primary importance. After each miracle the
Evangelist emphasizes the fact that the disciples did
not understand its true meaning (vi. 52 and viii. 17–
21) ; perhaps he means us to infer that they came to
a full recognition of the meaning of the " mystery of
the loaves " only after their eyes had been opened
near Cæsarea Philippi ; or, more probably, he thinks
(with St. John, xvi. 12–15, etc.) that they perceived
the significance of these " signs " only after the resurrection and the coming of the Spirit. But at any rate
he assumes that his readers, who understand the
narrative in the light of the resurrection-faith, will
perceive in the action of the Lord in feeding the multitudes the veiled reality of the Messiahship, and that
to those who have experienced the power of His
resurrection the Lord will be known in the breaking
of the bread (Luke xxiv. 35). A subsidiary implication
of Mark viii. 14–21 is that Christians need have no

anxiety concerning their daily bread ; they need take no thought about what they shall eat, since their Father knoweth that they have need of such things and will not give them a stone : in the Father's house there is " bread enough and to spare " (Luke xv. 17); those broken pieces, which remained over after all had eaten and were filled, are the symbol of the inexhaustible spiritual food which is not diminished by being used.

The feeding miracles are to be understood as the acts or " signs " of the Messiah. A miracle of precisely this character might have been looked for in the " prophet like unto Moses " (Deut. xviii. 15 ff.); St. John makes this point quite clear: " When the people saw the sign which He did, they said, This is of a truth the prophet that cometh into the world " (John vi. 14 ; cf. vi. 31–33, 49 f., 58 ; cf. Acts iii. 22). As Moses had dispensed bread from heaven in the wilderness, so Jesus in the desert distributes the Bread of Life. Elisha also had fed one hundred men with twenty loaves of barley (in John vi. 9 the loaves are said to be of barley), so that " they did eat and left thereof " (2 Kings iv. 42–44). It was appropriate that Jesus, Who stood between Moses and Elijah [1] on the Mount of Transfiguration, and Who had come to *fulfil* the Law and the Prophets, should authenticate His mission by means of the signs which they had given. The disciples, it is implied, ought to have understood the " mystery " which the sign of the Broken Bread reveals.

The introduction of the symbol of the fishes along with that of the loaves is not entirely explicable by us ;

[1] Elisha, upon whom Elijah's mantle had fallen, must be regarded as the shadow of which Elijah is the substance.

95

but we know that the symbol of fish was widely used as a "sign" amongst the earliest Christian communities. Since the original Galilæan disciples numbered several fishermen in their company, and since the fishing industry of the district was so important, it was appropriate that fish, along with bread, should have been one of the "common things" by which the Lord chose to make Himself known to those who had eyes to see. Bread and fish appear frequently in early Christian frescoes in the catacombs as a symbol of the Eucharist (cf. W. Lowrie, *Christian Art and Archæology*, pp. 223 ff., cited by Rawlinson). (Cf. also for symbolic references to fish in the N.T. : Luke v. 1–11, xxiv. 42 f. ; John xxi. 1–14, esp. verse 13, according to which the Risen Christ distributes bread and fish to the disciples.)

The early Church undoubtedly saw in the feeding miracles a deep Eucharistic significance ; St. John, who tells us that the Feeding of the Five Thousand took place at Passover-time (John vi. 4), connects the miracle with his discourse upon "the true bread out of heaven" (vi. 32) and upon "eating the flesh of the Son of Man and drinking His blood" (vi. 51–59 ; cf. especially vi. 51, "the bread which I will give is my flesh"). But the language of Mark vi. 41 and viii. 6 (including the word εὐχαριστήσας in the latter verse) is so closely parallel to that of Mark xiv. 22 or 1 Cor. xi. 23 f. (the Last Supper : "He took," "He blessed" or "gave thanks," "He break," "He gave") that the coincidences could hardly be unintentional. St. Paul in 1 Cor. x. 3 f. declares that the manna and the water from the rock which Moses struck, the food and drink of the Israelites in the desert, were none other than Christ Himself. The Lord Who through the resurrection-faith is revealed to the believer in the breaking of bread, Who to-day in His Church gives to His followers at the Eucharist His body for food and His blood for wine, is none other than that same eternal Christ Who in olden times had sustained the Israelites on their desert pilgrimage, incarnate in this same historical Jesus Who satisfied the hungry multitudes in the wilderness, or Who distributed to His disciples in the upper room the bread and the cup, symbols of His body broken and His blood shed, by which the world's redemption is procured. This is the theology which lies behind the miracle-stories of the feedings in all four Gospels. It should therefore not surprise us to find that the feeding stories occupy a place of outstanding importance in St. Mark's presentation of the Gospel narrative, or that the tradition of the Feeding of the Multitude was so deeply embedded in the evangelical witness : the story of the Feeding of the Five Thousand is the only miracle-story which appears (in a recognizably similar form) in all four Gospels, and the story of a feeding is told in the Gospels no less than six times.

It is entirely unnecessary to suppose that St. Mark's second story of the Feeding of the Multitude is only a " doublet " of the first, or that he carelessly incorporated a variant of the Feeding of the Five Thousand, which he had come across in the tradition, or that the second story did not belong to the original draft of the Gospel. The truth is rather that in telling the two separate stories he is symbolizing the offering of salvation " to the Jew first, but also to the Greek " (Rom. i. 16). He wishes to impart teaching concerning the Lord Who makes " no distinction between Jew and Greek," and Who, being " Lord of all," is " rich unto all that call upon Him " (Rom. x. 12). From the time of St. Augustine the suggestion has been known that

97

the Feeding of the Five Thousand represents Christ's communication of Himself to the Jews, and that of the Four Thousand represents His self-communication to the Gentiles (cf. Trench, *Notes on the Miracles*, p. 384 footnote). The disciples need have no anxiety concerning Christ's ability to supply spiritual food to the whole Gentile world. The scene of the Feeding of the Five Thousand suggests a Galilæan (*i.e.* Jewish) crowd ; that of the Feeding of the Four Thousand suggests a crowd drawn from the neighbourhood of the Decapolis (cf. Mark vii. 31) on the south-eastern side of the Sea of Galilee, *i.e.* a Gentile crowd. The Five Thousand receive the five loaves (possibly a reminiscence of the Five Books of the Law) ; the Four Thousand receive seven loaves (cf. the seventy nations into which the Gentile world was traditionally divided, the Septuagint, the Seven Deacons of Acts vi. 3, and St. Luke's Mission of the Seventy, Luke x. 1 ff.). At the former miracle twelve baskets are taken up, representing the Twelve Tribes of Israel (cf. Matt. xix. 28) ; at the latter, seven baskets remain over (cf. the above references). In the earlier story the word used for " basket " is κόφινος (Mark vi. 43), apparently a distinctively Jewish type of basket (Rawlinson, *St. Mark*, p. 87, says that the word occurs in Juvenal, iii. 14 and vi. 542 to denote a basket commonly used by the poorer class of Jews in Rome); in the second story the word for " basket " is σφυρίς (Mark viii. 8), an ordinary kind of basket, or fish-basket. That the distinction between the two words is not merely accidental is shown by its reappearance in Mark viii. 19 f. In view of this wealth of accumulative evidence it is impossible to doubt that St. Mark intended his readers to understand the interpretation of the feeding miracles which has been suggested above.

The purpose of that whole section of St. Mark's Gospel which we may entitle " The Opening of the Blind Eyes " (vi. 30–viii. 30) is now seen clearly to be that of displaying Jesus as the Christ, the signs of Whose coming were foretold in the Old Testament, and which are now supremely fulfilled in the miracle-stories of this section. Each of these stories plays its own important part in the development of this theme, so that when we reach the climax of viii. 27–30 (the Opening of St. Peter's Eyes) there can be no holding back from the full confession, " Thou art the Christ." The Lord Who is revealed to us in the miracle-stories is the Christ Who was known by promise in the Scriptures, the Deliverer to Whom the Law and the Prophets alike bear witness. Thus, the proper subject of the Old Testament, as of the New, is Christ, Who opens to us the Scriptures, interpreting the things concerning Himself. So Tertullian, arguing against the Marcionites, who wished to cut loose the New Testament from the Old, points to Elisha's miracle as pre-figuring the Offering of the Bread of Life by Christ, and continues :

> " O Christ ! even in Thy newness Thou art old. And so when Peter saw those things, and compared them with the things that had gone before, and had recognized that they were not merely things done in time past, but also even then were prophecies of the future, he on behalf of all men answered the Lord's question, ' Whom say ye that I am ? ' with the words, ' Thou art the Christ ' ; he could not but have perceived that He was the Christ, unless he had failed to perceive that He Whom he was now agnizing in His works was He Whom he had known in the Scriptures." [1]

[1] *Adv. Marc.* iv. 21 ; quoted by Trench, *op. cit.* p. 293.

CHAPTER VI

MIRACLE-STORIES IN THE LATER GOSPEL TRADITION

1. *St. Mark's Handling of the Miracle-Stories*

IT will now be apparent that St. Mark uses stories of miracles as vehicles by means of which instruction and exhortation may be conveyed. As we find them in his Gospel, the miracle-stories are the products of profound meditation upon the significance of the person and actions of Jesus, and their interest centres in their theological rather than in their historical character. They are neither the " reminiscences " of St. Peter or other eye-witnesses nor " tales " told by a secular order of story-tellers. Their motive is neither biographical nor literary ; they are the materials to be used by Christian preachers and teachers in their presentation of the Gospel. We have no reason to suppose that St. Mark was the first to discover that miracle-stories could be used in the task of instruction in the truths of the Gospel.

We have noticed, indeed, that the only miracle-story recorded in Q (the Centurion's Servant) is likewise made an instrument of the Church's teaching concerning the faith of the Gentile world. It is worth remarking also that the miracle-stories of the early chapters of Acts are used in precisely the same way as a means of expounding or illustrating the doctrines of the Church's faith (see *e.g.* Acts iii. 1–10, which becomes the basis of St. Peter's sermon which follows).

It is a reasonable hypothesis to suppose that St. Mark found miracle-stories already in use by the Church's teachers for the same purposes as those to which he has himself applied them in his Gospel. It is just those very miracle-stories which St. Mark already found in use in the tradition that he has preserved for us, and the authority of the miracle-story tradition does not depend upon one man, St. Mark, or upon one eye-witness, St. Peter, but is, on the contrary, the authority of the Church in Rome a generation after the crucifixion of the Lord. How far the Evangelist has adapted the tradition which he received to suit his own purposes it is, of course, impossible to determine ; but a conservative view is probably entirely justified here, in view of the solidarity of the Marcan theology and outlook with that of St. Paul and the other writers of the New Testament generally. We cannot look upon St. Mark as in any sense an innovator ; he is rather the preserver and scribe of the tradition in which he himself has been instructed.

Doubtless the manner in which the miracle-stories have been used in St. Mark's Gospel, particularly in vi. 30–viii. 30, which contributes so skilfully to the development of his theme, owes a great deal to the insight and artistry of the Evangelist himself ; but we may point out that even the Fourth Gospel supports the view that the mainstream of the Gospel tradition had from the beginning perceived the symbolic significance of the arrangement of the material from the Feeding of the Five Thousand to the Confession of St. Peter. We cannot tell how far the symbolism of the twice-attempted opening of the disciples' eyes, culminating in the Marcan stories of the Deaf-Mute and the Blind Man of Bethsaida, is St. Mark's own work, or how much of it was already found by him in the accepted tradition of the Church ; and we must be content to leave the matter there. But of this we may be assured : our earliest Gospel tells us nothing of a time when the miracles of the Lord were regarded as simple events devoid of theological interpretation, or when they were treated as illustrations of His wonderful power and compassion. The fact is that the theological or Christological significance which the stories carried not merely accounts for their preservation in the actual preaching and teaching tradition, but actually conditions the form in which the stories themselves came to be told. But how far this " conditioning " of the form of the stories as we find them in St. Mark's Gospel is due to the Evangelist himself and how much to those from whom he derived his material we cannot precisely tell.

It is probable, however, that one feature of the Marcan miracle-stories is due to the hand of the Evangelist himself, namely, the command to secrecy after the performance of some of the miracles. (This subject is fully dealt with by Prof. R. H. Lightfoot, *History and Interpretation*, pp. 67 ff., *q.v.*) St. Mark is grappling with the problem of Rom. ix.-xi., how the Jewish people, who received Christ in the flesh, could yet reject Him. (Cf. Mark iv. 10–25, vi. 1–6.) The Evangelist's answer is given on the plane of history by the suggestion that Jesus Himself imposed silence upon those for whom miracles of a Messianic significance had been wrought. He commands the dæmons (who recognize Who He is) to be silent (i. 25, 34 ; iii. 11 f.), and in four miracle-stories which are not exorcisms the command to silence is also given (the Leper, i. 44 ; Jairus's Daughter, v. 43 ; the Deaf-Mute, vii. 36 ;

and the Blind Man of Bethsaida, viii. 26). All these miracles are of Messianic import, and it is understandable that St. Mark should conceive it to be appropriate to insert the command to secrecy at these points. But he has not worked out his theory very carefully, since in some sections of his Gospel he appears to have overlooked it (cf. esp. Mark ii. 1–12 and 28). This merely shows that St. Mark is more interested in the theological implications of the matter than in the construction of a consistent historical narrative or of a neatly-finished literary biography. The recognition of this state of affairs is not so conducive to a purely sceptical estimate of the possibility of our knowledge of the historical Jesus as it might at first be supposed ; but the discussion of this question would take us beyond the limits of our subject.

2. St. Matthew's Handling of the Miracle-Stories

The statement, frequently encountered, that St. Matthew generally " heightens the miraculous effect " in his treatment of the Marcan material must be received with caution. As we have noticed,[1] St. Matthew does not intend to modify St. Mark's statement, " He could there do no mighty work, save that He laid His hands on a few sick folk and healed them " (Mark vi. 5), since St. Mark did not mean what a number of modern critics have assumed him to mean ; St. Matthew is only abbreviating, as is his custom, when he says, " He did not many mighty works there because of their unbelief " (xiii. 58)— which is precisely what St. Mark intends. Again, St. Matthew is concerned to render more compact St. Mark's " dovetailed " story of the Barren Fig-tree, and is thus led to declare that the fig-tree withered

[1] Cf. *supra*, p. 44.

"immediately" (xxi. 19) instead of on the next day (Mark xi. 20). The "miraculous effect" itself, however, is hardly "heightened," since the shortening of the time does not make the event *per se* more extraordinary ; indeed, St. Matthew does not go so far as St. Mark in saying that the tree was withered "from the roots." Similarly St. Matthew's tendency to substitute two blind men or two demoniacs (xx. 30 and viii. 28) instead of one hardly makes the miracle any more wonderful, and is doubtless due to his desire to provide a more literal fulfilment of prophecy, as in the case of the two asses at the Triumphal Entry (xxi. 2, 7). Everywhere St. Matthew is concerned to emphasize the fulfilment of the prophecies concerning the days of the Messiah, as, for instance, in his generalized accounts of the healing of the lame, the blind, the dumb and the maimed (xv. 29–31, xxi. 14 ; cf. xiv. 34–36). After recording the healing at eventide (cf. Mark i. 32–34) he adds a further reflection upon the fulfilment of prophecy : Jesus healed the sick and the demoniacs, he says, "that it might be fulfilled which was spoken by Isaiah the prophet, saying, Himself took our infirmities and bare our diseases" (Matt. viii. 17 ; cf. Isa. liii. 4 f.). It is clear that St. Matthew is anxious to reassert and re-emphasize the Messianic significance of the miracles of the Lord, and in this respect his attitude towards the miracle-stories of the Gospel tradition is in harmony with that of all the other Evangelists.

In the opening section of the Gospel (the Birth-Narratives) St. Matthew specially stresses the fulfilment of prophecy by miraculous means (i. 18–ii. 23) ; but the prophecy-motive is not apparent in the miraculous phenomena which he introduces into the Passion Story

(Pilate's Wife's Dream, xxvii. 19 ; the Earthquake and the Opening of the Tombs, xxvii. 51–53 ; and the Setting of a Guard, xxvii. 62–66). These latter details, which Bacon refers to as " apocryphal supplements " (*Studies in Matthew*, p. 258), resemble the use of the miraculous in the Apocryphal Gospels more nearly than anything else in the Canonical Gospels, since here the main motives behind the use of miracle-stories on the part of the Four Evangelists seem to be lacking. According to Matt. xxvii. 54 it was, in part at least, the earthquake which caused the centurion and the other bystanders to say, " Truly this was (the) Son of God." This is, of course, just the way in which the miraculous element is *not* used throughout the rest of the Canonical Gospels. It is conspicuous by its absence as well in St. Matthew as in the other three Gospels.

St. Matthew adds no clear and distinct miracle-story to those narrated by St. Mark (except the Q story of the Centurion's Servant). His additions to the Marcan miracle-narratives are, in Streeter's words, " parasitic ; they stand to Mark as mistletoe to the oak." [1] They resemble the Rabbinic Haggada of Old Testament stories. B. W. Bacon, agreeing with Streeter's view, says [2] that no Jew would ever have asked if such edificatory embellishments as " the midrash of the coin in the fish's mouth " were *true* stories. They were intended as " pure haggadic fable when first related to a Christian ' synagogue.' " The stories of St. Peter's Walking on the Sea (Matt. xiv. 28–31) and the Coin in the Fish's Mouth (Matt. xvii. 24–27) are classified by Bacon (along with the *Tu es Petrus* passage of Matt. xvi. 17–19) as the

[1] *The Four Gospels*, p. 502.
[2] *Studies in Matthew*, p. 229.

"Petrine Supplements" of the Fourth Book of Matthew (*i.e.* Matt. xiii. 54–xix. 1*a*). These Petrine Supplements, which occur in no other part of the Gospel, are devoted to the support of the unique authority of St. Peter in the Church. In the first of them, St. Peter's Walking on the Sea, the historical truth that the Church was founded upon the faith of St. Peter, rather than on that of any other individual, is symbolically expressed (cf. xvi. 17–19). St. Peter had boldly offered to stay by his Master to the end, to brave the storm of persecution and hatred, but his courage failed him—he began to sink, till Jesus "took hold of him."

This interpretation of the Matthæan addition to the Marcan *pericope* is strengthened if, as Loisy, Bacon and others have thought, there is a symbolic significance underlying the *order* of the stories in the Gospel tradition, according to which the Feeding of the Five Thousand is followed by the Walking on the Sea (Mark vi. 30–52, Matt. xiv. 13–33, John vi. 1–21). The Feeding symbolizes Jesus's farewell to His disciples at the Last Supper ; the withdrawal from them, when they enter the boat, represents His separation from them by His death and burial ; and the Walking on the Sea denotes the return of the Lord to the disciples in the resurrection. The part played by St. Peter in the resurrection narratives—his "turning again" and the "strengthening" of his brethren (Luke xxii. 32)—is then clearly symbolized in the Matthæan story of his attempt to walk on the sea, in which he succeeds through the power of Christ, after his initial failure. The very faith of Peter on which the Church is built (Matt. xvi. 18) is itself but a fragile thing, which must depend always upon Christ and not upon any human capacity—St. Peter is he to whom the words are spoken : "O thou of little faith." Faith which is only self-reliance and not reliance upon Christ is impotent.

The story of the Coin in the Fish's Mouth (Matt. xvii. 24–27) is not strictly a miracle-story, for, though a miracle is doubtless implied, none is explicitly affirmed. Some have classed it as a paradigm or pronouncement-story,[1] since it contains a saying bearing upon a problem of conscience which confronted the early Jewish-Christian community. The latter had to meet the practical question as to whether they should pay the capitation tax (κῆνσος), levied upon all Jews, for the maintenance of the Temple. This was distinct from the " custom " (τέλη) collected on behalf of the Roman government by the *publicani*. After A.D. 70 the tax still continued, but it was appropriated by the Romans. We learn from the *pericope* that Jesus Himself paid the Temple tax (Matt. xvii. 24 f.), but that He had said that His disciples, as children of the Father's house, ought to receive in this matter the freedom (*i.e.* exemption) of sons (xvii. 26). Perhaps we may infer from the story that Jewish-Christians before A.D. 70 were in the habit of paying the Temple tax " under protest." After A.D. 70, when the state had taken over the tax, Jewish-Christians would pay it on the principle laid down in Mark xii. 13–17 (" Render unto Cæsar . . .") and defined by St. Paul in Rom. xiii. 7 (" Render to all their dues . . ."). It may well be that an original " pronouncement-story " concluded with the saying of verse 26 : " Therefore the sons are free," and that the legendary verse 27

[1] *E.g.* F. W. Green, *St. Matthew*, p. 212. If the story was an original paradigm, why is the teaching of verses 25 f. said to be given privately in the house ?

was added after A.D. 70 in order to justify the practice of the Jewish-Christians, who regularly paid the tax. But this is only conjecture.

The significance of the fact that Jesus Himself paid taxes, whether to the Jewish Church or the Roman State, should not be overlooked. As Sin-Bearer, He is implicated in the whole sinful complex of human social relationships, whether of the State or of the Church (as a human, empirical organization). He pays the tax which, while it aids in the maintenance of law and order in society, at the same time upholds a tyrannical government, which denies individual freedom and social justice. The whole problem of the Christian's involvement as a citizen in the sin of the society from which he cannot escape is focused in the incarnation of the Lord Who, though He knew no sin, was made to be sin for us (2 Cor. v. 21).

3. *St. Luke's Handling of the Miracle-Stories*

St. Luke, like St. Matthew, reproduces most of the Marcan miracle-stories without substantially altering their form or their meaning. In some stories (the Epileptic Boy, for example, Mark ix. 14–29, Matt. xvii. 14–20, Luke ix. 37–43) St. Matthew and St. Luke have abbreviated the narrative to such an extent that St. Mark's version looks like a later literary elaboration of their simpler and more original forms.[1] In general, it may be said that while St. Matthew

[1] If the Form-Critics based their judgments upon "form" alone, they would have to maintain that the Lucan story of the Epileptic Boy is the original, for it exhibits the miracle-story form to perfection. It concludes, as Mark does not, with an expression of astonishment on the part of the bystanders : "They were all astonished at the majesty (μεγαλειότητι) of God " (Luke ix. 43). This conclusion is a more categorical affirmation of the meaning of the miracles of Jesus than anything which we find in Mark. (Cf. also Luke xviii. 43 with Mark x. 52).

and St. Luke follow in the footsteps of St. Mark in using the miracle-stories to illustrate the Church's teaching concerning the person of Christ, the symbolic use to which they have put them is less elaborate than that which we have discovered in St. Mark. St. Luke's "Great Omission" (*i.e.* of the entire section, Mark vi. 45–viii. 26) completely spoils the symbolism of the stages of the Opening of the Disciples' Eyes in Mark vi. 30–viii. 30 ; and St. Matthew does not seem to have noticed it. In general, it may be said that St. Luke, like St. Matthew, shares the attitude of St. Mark to the miracle-stories ; the later Synoptists bring no new motives or didactic purposes to the telling of the miracle-stories beyond those which we have already discovered in our examination of the miracle-narratives of St. Mark.

If any exception should be made to this statement, it would be that of the so-called Petrine Supplements of Matthew, to which there is a remarkable parallel in the Lucan story of the Miraculous Draught of Fishes (Luke v. 1–11). A non-Marcan motive in these stories seems to be the drawing of attention to St. Peter's place of prominence in the apostolic band. Whether St. Luke's story of the Draught of Fishes is derived from the same cycle of Petrine traditions as the Matthæan Petrine Supplements it is impossible to say. There seems to have been a story of this kind which both St. Luke and St. John had come across, for a variant of it appears in John xxi. 1–14. In some respects the Johannine version appears to be the more primitive ; for instance, the miracle is not so stupendous as in Luke, where the haul is so great as to break the nets and capsize the boats. St. John's setting of the narrative as a resurrection-story appears to be more appropriate to its general character. It has been suggested that St. Luke derived the story

from the Lost Ending of St. Mark (Harnack) ; others
have thought that it was created out of the saying about
" fishers of men " (Mark i. 17) (Wellhausen). It is
clear that St. Luke combined whatever material he may
have found with details from Mark i. 16–20 and iv. 1.
Whatever may have been the origin of the story, its
significance for St. Luke, the historian of the early
Church, is obvious : St. Peter as the *primus* and leader
of the early Church is called by the Lord to be a fisher
of men ; and the success of the Church's missionary
enterprise under his leadership is foreshadowed by the
miraculous haul of fishes ; when Peter first puts forth
at Jesus's command and under His direction, so many
converts are made that the Church's organization and
resources are strained to breaking-point. The Christian
missionary must always be ready to follow the guidance
of the Lord, and to go where he is sent ; it is only
through the help of Christ that success is attained ; and
thus the story contains both instruction and encouragement for a missionary Church in every age.

Apart from the story of the Miraculous Draught
of Fishes (Luke v. 1–11), there are four miracle-
stories proper which are peculiar to St. Luke.[1]
These are : the Raising of the Widow's Son at Nain
(vii. 11–17), the Woman Healed on the Sabbath
(xiii. 10–17), the Dropsical Man Healed on the
Sabbath (xiv. 1–6) and the Ten Lepers (xvii. 11–19).[2]
In all these stories the motives and theological
implications are those which we find in the Marcan

[1] St. Luke's attitude to the miraculous may also be studied in his
birth- and resurrection-stories, which fall outside the scope of our
discussion, and in Acts. The latter contains some sixteen recorded
miracles, amongst which are six excellent specimens of the miracle-
story " form," and eight general editorial accounts of the typical
miracles of the Apostles.

[2] In addition, St. Luke is the only one of the Evangelists to record
the detail of the healing of the wounded ear of the high priest's servant
(xxii. 51).

miracle-stories, and no new motives appear—except perhaps in one instance, the subsidiary motive of St. Luke's interest in the Samaritans (xvii. 16), whose attitude (as elsewhere in the Gospel, cf. Luke x. 30–37) is contrasted favourably with that of the Jews. It has been urged by some that St. Luke has derived these stories from a special source, but all of them are so reminiscent of the Marcan cycle of miracle-narratives that it appears more probable that St. Luke has constructed them himself out of Marcan materials. It is hard to escape the conclusion, especially if we have regard to some of the miracle-stories of Acts, that St. Luke did not hesitate to construct such stories, in harmony alike with the main purpose and general content of the Church's tradition, in order the better to illustrate the significance of the work of Jesus or the preaching of the Apostles by means of teaching conveyed in story form. The stories would thus represent the truth of the Gospel, the truth about Jesus and the Apostles, as the Church understood it, even though they are not to be regarded as necessarily accurate recordings of specific historical happenings.[1]

Two of the miracles peculiar to St. Luke deal with the familiar evangelical theme of Sabbath-

[1] The evidence from the vocabulary of these four stories is not decisive, but it hardly supports the view (as Creed seems to suppose, *The Gospel according to St. Luke*, pp. 103 f.) that St. Luke derived them from a special source. The peculiarly Lucan designation of Jesus as ὁ κύριος in two of these stories (vii. 13, xiii. 15) is found elsewhere in Luke in passages peculiar to that Gospel or in introductions which St. Luke has furnished to other material (cf. vii. 19, x. 1, 39, 41, xi. 39, xii. 42, xvii. 5, xviii. 6, xix. 8, xxii. 31, 61, xxiv. 3). It is not found in narrative passages in Mark or Matthew. In Luke xvii. 13 we find the word ἐπιστάτα, the Lucan substitute for ῥαββεί or διδάσκαλε.

healing. The first of these, the Woman Healed on the Sabbath (xiii. 10–17), is a story of Jesus's teaching in the Synagogue, which is hardly appropriate in the context of the journey to Jerusalem. It is reminiscent of the Marcan story of the Withered Hand (Mark iii. 1–6, which Luke reproduces in vi. 6–11) and also of the Woman with an Issue (Mark v. 25–34, reproduced in Luke viii. 43–48, without the damaging severity of St. Mark's words concerning the physicians !). The second story, that of the Dropsical Man (Luke xiv. 1–6), is also reminiscent of the Withered Hand [1] ; indeed, the saying, " Which of you shall have an ass or an ox fallen into a well, and will not straightway draw him up on a Sabbath day ? " (Luke xiv. 5) is actually incorporated by St. Matthew into his version of the Withered Hand (Matt. xii. 11). A similar saying is introduced by St. Luke into the story of the Woman Healed on the Sabbath : " Doth not each one of you on the Sabbath loose his ox or his ass from the stall and lead him away to watering ? " (xiii. 15). The story of the Ten Lepers (Luke xvii. 11–19) is reminiscent of St. Mark's story of the Leper (Mark i. 40–45, reproduced in Luke v. 12–16) ; indeed, it seems to be a version of it which is specially adapted for circulation in a non-Jewish Church. Jesus as Healer bestows His mercy on all who call upon Him, whether Jews or not ; but whereas the Jews are not grateful for the manifestation of the divine grace which has been vouchsafed to them, others are.

[1] Cf. Luke xiv. 1, " They were watching Him," with Mark iii. 2, " They watched Him, whether He would heal him on the Sabbath day."

The story of the Widow's Son at Nain (Luke vii.
11–17) is full of profound theological content. It
constitutes a Messianic sign, that of the raising of the
dead, to which Jesus refers in the following section,
the reply to John the Baptist's question : " the dead
are raised up " (vii. 22). It is a sign which John, as the
Elijah Redivivus, would surely recognize, for had not
Elijah, and Elisha after him, raised a widow's only
son from the dead (1 Kings xvii. 17–24, 2 Kings iv.
21–37) ? Indeed, the very scene of the giving of the
sign was full of meaning—the miracle tradition does
not usually contain place-names, which are irrelevant
to its purpose : Nain was near the ancient city of
Shunem, where Elisha's miracle had been performed.
The words of Luke vii. 15, καὶ ἔδωκεν αὐτὸν τῇ μητρὶ
αὐτοῦ, are identical with those of 1 Kings xvii. 23
(LXX). The exclamation of the bystanders, " A
great prophet is arisen among us " (Luke vii. 16),
indicates that they have correctly perceived the Old
Testament parallels,[1] and their further comment,
" God hath visited His people," [2] is an acknowledgment of the Messianic implication of the miracle,
which the disciples of John are to convey to their

---

[1] It is quite unnecessary to assume that this phrase dates back to
an early period when the Christology of the Church was undeveloped
and Jesus was regarded either as " a great prophet " or vaguely as
ὁ κύριος (cf. vii. 13). The use by St. Luke of the former phrase is
due solely to his desire to point out the parallel of Elijah-Elisha. A
precisely similar result occurs in John vi. 14, where St. John wishes
to call attention to the parallel with Moses : " This is the *prophet*
that cometh into the world."

[2] The phrase is similar to Luke i. 68, " He hath visited and wrought
redemption for His people," which St. Luke has probably taken from
a source. But it is interesting that at vii. 16, where (according to our
view) he is writing freely and not following a source, he omits the words
καὶ ἐποίησε λύτρωσιν, in accordance with his own theological outlook,
which does not stress the idea of redemption.

master. Finally, we should notice that the story is reminiscent of the Raising of Jairus's Daughter (Mark v. 21 ff., reproduced in Luke viii. 41 ff. ; cp. " Young man, I say unto thee, Arise " with " Damsel, I say unto thee, Arise "). The Marcan effect is now heightened : Jairus's Daughter has just died, but the Widow's Son is already on his way to the tomb ; in the Fourth Gospel, Lazarus has been dead four days (John xi. 39).

4. *St. John's Handling of the Miracle-Stories*

Any adequate consideration of the miracle-stories of the Fourth Gospel must include an attempt to show their relation to the general nature and specific purpose of that Gospel. All that we can hope to do here is to indicate briefly the grounds of our view that St. John stands in the general line of the development of the Synoptic tradition ; he introduces no new motives into the telling of miracle-stories ; he stresses and elaborates the old ones. There is no specifically " Johannine " interpretation of the miracle-stories. St. John agrees with the Synoptists that the miracles are not to be regarded as mere " wonders " ; he insists that they have a deep spiritual meaning. He never refers to them as τέρατα (except perhaps deprecatingly in iv. 48, his only use of the word) or even as δυνάμεις. He usually calls them σημεῖα, a word which he uses seventeen times. The miracles certainly attract the multitudes to Jesus (vi. 2, xii. 18 f.), and they are undoubtedly regarded as pointers to a living belief in the person of Christ (ii. 23, vii. 31); common honesty must compel the admission that such works could not be wrought by a sinner or apart from the power of God (cf. ix. 16, iii. 2) ; but the faith by which their true meaning is perceived is a gift of God (cf. xii. 37). Without this faith the miracles are profitless : " ye seek me, not because ye saw signs, but because ye ate of the loaves and were filled " (vi. 26). As Dr. W. Temple reminds us, " whenever we try to use our religion as a solution of our temporal problems, caring more for that than for God and His glory, we fall under the same condemnation." [1] This is the consistent teaching of the author of the Fourth Gospel. As we saw in our first chapter, the δόξα of Jesus is veiled, even in St. John, except from the eyes which have been opened to the Light. St. John shares the common New Testament attitude towards the veiling of the mystery of Christ in the present age.

The seven miracles recorded in the Fourth Gospel are : the Changing of the Water into Wine (ii. 1–11) ; the Healing of the Nobleman's Son (iv. 46–54) ; the Healing of the Impotent Man (v. 2–9) ; the Feeding of the Five Thousand (vi. 4–13) ; the Walking on the Water (vi. 16–21) ; the Healing of the Man Born Blind (ix. 1–7) ; and the Raising of Lazarus (xi. 1–44). The number seven is probably symbolic, and St. John implies that Jesus actually worked many more than seven miracles. The significance of some of these miracles is discussed at great length in the long speeches of Jesus or the controversies with His enemies, the Jews ; but it is to be noticed that each of these discussions is only an underlining or explication of the interpretation which we have seen to be already implicit in St. Mark. Although the importance of the stories is not to be found in the sheer magnitude of the miracle recorded, it is nevertheless true that all seven of St. John's miracles are stupendous feats of super-

[1] *Readings in St. John's Gospel*, First Series, pp. 83 f.

natural power, admitting of no naturalistic or rationalistic explanation. Even those which he shares with the Synoptists are the most astonishing which the latter record, such as the Feeding of the Five Thousand, the Walking on the Sea [1] and the Healing (at a distance) of the Nobleman's Son (which we take to be a variant of the Centurion's Servant). The Impotent Man (probably a variation of the theme of the Paralytic) has been afflicted for thirty-eight years, and St. John's Blind Man has been blind from birth. The nature miracle of the Changing of the Water into Wine involves the astounding feat of the creation of well over one hundred gallons of wine ; and Lazarus is brought back to life after he has been dead four days. Thus, even if St. John warns us against the danger of believing that the importance of the miracles resides in their impressiveness as wonders, he does not allow us to overlook the fact that the miracles of Jesus *were* miracles, and not mere symbolic actions which *any* prophet might have performed. They are " the works which none other did " (John xv. 24).

The difficulties of accepting the " historicity " of the Johannine miracle-stories, as is well known, are not occasioned merely by the stupendousness of the miracles which they record. It is no more incredible *per se* that Jesus should have raised Lazarus than that He should have raised Jairus's Daughter. Both events are alike

---

[1] It is surely unwarrantable to suppose (with Bernard, W. Temple, *op. cit.* p. 77, and others) that St. John minimizes the miraculous element in this sign on the grounds that the phrase ἐπὶ τῆς θαλάσσης (vi. 19) may possibly mean " by the sea," as it does in xxi. 1. Jesus " drew nigh unto the boat " when the disciples had rowed 25 or 30 furlongs (about 3½ miles) ; as the Sea of Galilee is about 7 miles across, St. John here gives an accurate gloss on Mark's " in the midst of the sea " ; so Hoskyns, *The Fourth Gospel*, i. pp. 327 f.

inexplicable. The real difficulty is that of believing that, had the Synoptists known of them, they would have refrained from relating them. No reason has ever been satisfactorily put forward to account for the fact that the Synoptists, had they known of them, should not have recorded Jesus's first miracle at Cana, or the raising of Lazarus at Bethany, which so vitally affected (according to John) the course of events in Passion Week. It is equally difficult to believe that they would not have heard of these public occurrences. Upon this problem there exists a vast literature, and it is not our purpose at this point to enter further into the discussion of the whole question of the historicity of the Fourth Gospel which it raises.

Sometimes St. John takes the miracle-stories and brings out their meaning by introducing into them long and elaborate discussions between Jesus and the Jews concerning their Christological implications (*e.g.* John ix. or xi.). In other cases the implications of the miracle are brought out in a later section of the Gospel. The implications of the miracle at Cana, along with those of Jesus's other " sign," the Cleansing of the Temple (ii. 13–22), are discussed in the long conversation with Nicodemus in iii. 1–21. The significance of the Walking on the Sea is not elaborated until we reach the 'long discourse of Jesus to the disciples in chh. xiii.–xvi. The latter story and the other Marcan narrative, the Feeding of the Five Thousand, are related in substantially their traditional form, but in such a way as to develop more clearly their symbolic allusion (which doubtless they had all along been perceived to contain) to the Lord's withdrawal from the disciples at the crucifixion and His return to them at the resurrection. The connexion between the Feeding and the event in the Upper

Room on the night in which Jesus was betrayed is suggested in vi. 4 : " Now the Passover, the feast of the Jews, was at hand." The " darkness over all the land " (Mark xv. 33) at the crucifixion is symbolized by the reference to the darkness in which the disciples laboured when Jesus had not yet come to them (John vi. 17 ; cf. xiii. 30). The Eucharistic significance of the feeding miracle, which, as we have noted, is already fully implicit in St. Mark's account, is carefully elaborated in the so-called Eucharistic Discourse of John vi. 22 ff. St. John's commentary upon the inner meaning of the Walking on the Sea is, however, reserved for treatment in subsequent passages of the Gospel in which Jesus speaks of His going away to return again (" If I go and prepare a place for you, I come again and will receive you unto myself," xiv. 3 ; " I will not leave you desolate : I come unto you," xiv. 18 ; cf. also xvi. 5–7, 16–22).

If the story of the Nobleman's Son (John iv. 46–54) is based upon the Q story (as we find it in Matt. viii. 5–13 and Luke vii. 1–10) of the Centurion's Servant, it is obvious that the universalist implications of the latter are not now regarded as of importance ; that battle was already a story of yesterday when St. John wrote. Even the great saying of Jesus regarding the faith of the Gentiles has disappeared, and the Nobleman is presumably himself a Jew. The point of the story, as St. John tells it, is concerned rather with faith and its nature ; our human distress may drive us to seek the blessings which flow from Christ through faith in Him, yet faith which is only a desire for the blessings associated with faith is not true faith (iv. 48), but only the threshold to it (iv. 53).[1] The miracles of

[1] Cf. Hoskyns, *The Fourth Gospel*, i. pp. 288 f.

Jesus are " signs " (iv. 54) only to those who already have faith to understand them as the acts of Christ. This is, however, as we have seen, the attitude of all the Gospel-writers towards the miracles which they relate ; it is not a peculiarly " Johannine " interpretation of them.

Immediately after the story of the Nobleman's Son, St. John gives us his account of the Healing of the Impotent Man at the Bethesda Pool in Jerusalem (v. 1–18). This story bears affinities to that of the Paralytic (Mark ii. 1–12), with which it is undoubtedly connected.[1] As St. Mark has developed in his story the implication of Jesus's act of healing in the sphere of forgiveness, so St. John in the long discourse which follows (v. 19–47) elaborates the same theme of the ἐξουσία which the Father has given to the Son (v. 27). St. John also introduces into the narrative (as he does into the story of the Man Born Blind, ix. 14 ff.) the question concerning Sabbath-healings (v. 10, 16–18), which we have seen to be a common motive of the Synoptic miracle-story tradition.

Similarly the long story of the Healing of the Man Born Blind (John ix.) is an elaboration of the theme of Mark viii. 22–26 or x. 46–52 (the Blind Man of Bethsaida and Bartimæus). The causing of the lame to walk and the opening of the eyes of the blind are eschatological miracles, foretold by the prophets, whose significance is not lost upon the Jews (John v. 18, ix. 22). Throughout the discussions of ch. ix., St. John is concerned to elaborate the great truths which St. Mark has been content to leave implicit in his narrative. Christ is the Light of the world,

---

[1] Cf. "Arise, take up thy bed (κράββατον) and walk," Mark ii. 9, John v. 8—almost verbally identical.

by which men are led from darkness and error to faith and sight. The story of the Raising of Lazarus (John xi. 1–46) illustrates in a similar fashion the truth that Christ is the resurrection and the life of all the faithful. To those who know Christ, the resurrection is not merely a hope for the future but a present reality. St. Mark in the story of Jairus's Daughter and St. Luke in the story of the Widow's Son have dealt with the same essential theme, and there is a Q saying which indicates that Jesus Himself claimed to have raised the dead ; but the nearest Synoptic parallel to the Johannine story is the parable of Dives and Lazarus (Luke xvi. 19–31). In this parable it is concluded that the Jews, who have not listened to Moses and the prophets, would not be persuaded if Lazarus were to rise from the dead. In John xi. this parable has become a literal event : Lazarus does in fact rise from the dead, and the Jews are not persuaded. But for St. John it is not the mere *event* which is of chief importance, but the truth which it symbolizes : Lazarus (like the Impotent Man or the Man Born Blind) is the type or symbol of the whole human race, man as such : the Lord must re-create our humanity ; He must raise us up to resurrection life, He must open our eyes to the Light which shines in Him, and He must restore our disabled powers in order that we may stand upon our feet and walk. For the life of unredeemed man is only a living death ; his eyes are blinded from his birth in sin, and he cannot see the truth ; he is impotent to help himself. Christ is the restorer of our true humanity.

The story of the Changing of the Water into Wine (John ii. 1–11), it must be admitted, is unlike anything in the Synoptic tradition. The difficulty of believing that St. John intended us to take it literally is not the mere size of the miracle involved, for that in itself could be no stumbling-block to those who believe that Christ is the power of God, but rather its somewhat unreasonable character. We must frankly face the difficulty that to create such a quantity of good wine " when men have drunk freely " is hardly an act of common sense, and makes a poor " beginning of miracles " for the Good Teacher of the Christian tradition. On the other hand, the story carries some highly suggestive symbolism, and there is a sense in which the whole Gospel is a commentary upon it. Along with the following " sign " of the Cleansing of the Temple (ii. 13–22) it forms an introduction to the discourse with Nicodemus (iii. 1–21), in which the ruler of the Jews is shown the inadequacy of Judaism and the necessity of a re-birth through Christ. The meaning of the miracle at Cana is that Judaism must be purified (cf. ii. 6) and transformed in order to find its fulfilment in Christ, the bringer of new life, the eternal life of God, now offered to the world through His Son. The truth is known only to those who do His will (" the servants who drew the water knew," ii. 9 ; cf. vii. 17).

It is conceivably possible that in this story St. John is deliberately correcting a misinterpretation of a saying which has found its way into the Synoptic tradition— the saying added by St. Luke (v. 39) to the Marcan saying about the new wine and the old wine-skins : " No man having drunk old (wine) desireth new, for, he saith, the old is good (or *better*, R.V. margin)." St. John, who throughout his Gospel is concerned to demonstrate the superiority of Christianity over Judaism, may be guarding here against the misapplication of this saying by the Judaizers, who taught that the old wine of Judaism was superior to the new wine of Christianity. On the contrary, says St. John, Judaism is but the water of purification from which Christ makes the wine of eternal life.

CHAPTER VII

THE HISTORICAL AND RELIGIOUS VALUE OF THE MIRACLE-STORIES

1. " *Did the Miracles Really Happen?* "

THE consideration of the miracle-stories of the Fourth Gospel has brought us inescapably face to face with the question of the historical value of the whole miracle-story tradition in the Gospels. Did Jesus really work miracles? Did He indeed walk on the sea, change water into wine, or raise Lazarus from the dead? The miracle-stories of St. John's Gospel raise the question of history in an acute form, but we must notice that the question is raised not merely by the latest Gospel but by the earliest. When we read St. Mark's Gospel, we are confronted by the question whether Jesus made a paralytic walk, or raised Jairus's daughter, or healed a leper. What is probably our oldest documentary source reveals that Jesus Himself claimed to have healed the blind, the lame, the lepers and the deaf, and to have raised the dead (Q, Matt. xi. 5, Luke vii. 22). Jesus Himself confronts us with this question about miracle. " When I brake the five loaves among the five thousand, how many baskets full of broken pieces took ye up? " (Mark viii. 19 f.). Jesus stands in the middle of history and asks us a question about the meaning of history : " Do ye not yet understand ? "

We must now try, at the end of our investigation

of the New Testament understanding of the meaning of the miracle-stories, to answer the question which we could not answer at the beginning. We have now a better chance of satisfactorily answering the question about history, because we have come to see more clearly what history is. History is not merely a recording of facts, but an interpretation of facts as well. Chronicling facts is not the same thing as history-writing, for the latter involves the *selection* of the facts which are deemed to be of the greatest importance and the *interpretation* of those facts in the light of the total outlook and philosophy of the historian. Thus, history (*i.e.* the *record* of events in past time, not the series of events themselves, which as such we can never know absolutely) is a matter of selection and interpretation of facts.[1] This is exactly what the Gospel-writers have done for us : they have selected and interpreted the facts. Sometimes it is said that the Evangelists are not primarily historians but theologians ; but this is a half-truth which is apt to be misleading: they have fulfilled exactly the proper task of the historian : they have given us a selection and interpretation of certain facts which they thought to be of crucial importance. They are not chroniclers ; they have not attempted to catalogue all the things which Jesus ever said or ever did, and if they had tried to do this, they would have been attempting the impossible : " There are also many other things which

---

[1] The word " history " is, of course, equivocal, meaning either the sequence of events as they occurred or the record of those events as they have been remembered and written down. It is chiefly in the latter sense that the word is used in the following pages, although the former sense is quite legitimate, as when we speak of an event as being " historical," meaning nothing more than that it really happened.

Jesus did, the which, if they should be written every one, I suppose that even the world itself would not contain the books that should be written " (John xxi. 25). Thus, the Evangelists have not told us a great number of the facts about Jesus which a modern biographer would have put into his first chapter. They are concerned to give us only those facts which seem to them to be essential to the understanding of the mystery of Who Jesus is. They have selected the most significant facts and neglected others which, though we might have been very interested in them, were not relevant to the purpose which they had in hand. They are historians who—as all historians must do—have selected their facts and given to them their interpretation, with the result that, if we do not accept that interpretation, we become sceptical about the very possibility of our knowledge of the facts themselves.[1] If we had access to a history of Jesus written by some contemporary unbeliever, it would then have been possible to believe in a historical Jesus Who was *not* the Son of God, the worker of miracles and the vanquisher of the tomb ; but we have no such history, and therefore the only historical view remains that of the Evangelists, and the only alternative to it is a complete scepticism concerning the possibility of our knowledge of Jesus at all. The one thing which we cannot do is to invent a picture of Jesus which professes to be based upon the " facts " which the Evangelists record yet ignores their interpretation of them, for fact and interpretation are indissoluble and together constitute " history." A Jesus Who is not

[1] I have dealt with this point at greater length in an article in *Theology*, vol. xl. No. 238 (April 1940), entitled *Biblical Theology and the Modern Mood*.

the object of the faith of St. Mark and St. Paul and St. John is very soon exposed as the creation of our modern imagination.

The history which the Evangelists write is their good news, their Gospel. They believed that in Jesus of Nazareth God had spoken His saving Word to the world. If we accept their Gospel, we accept the history which they record, and we do not find it difficult to believe with them that the *form* of the revelation which God made in Christ included the working of the " signs " which proclaimed to the opened eyes the fulfilment of the age-long hope of the prophets of Israel, the promise that God would visit and redeem His people. If we reject that Gospel, we shall inevitably reject the view that Jesus performed miracles, or we shall seek to explain them away by means of the hypothesis of " faith-healing " or other modern theories equally removed from the standpoint of the biblical theology. The truth is that, as we have all along maintained, the miracle-stories are a part of the Gospel itself ; Christ is to the New Testament writers the manifestation of the power of God in the world, and His mighty deeds are the signs of the effectual working of that power. But in this age the power of God is veiled ; revelation is by the gift of faith. It is possible for us to fail to see Christ as the manifestation of the power and the purpose of God ; then we shall be content with an explanation of the miracle-stories in terms of modern psychology or folk-mythology. The miracle-stories, as an essential part of the preaching of apostolic Christianity, confront us with the question whether the power of God was or was not revealed in the person and work of Jesus Christ. They compel us to say Yes or No.

" History " cannot be detached from theology in such a way that the miracle-stories (or indeed any other part of the Gospel tradition, such as the " teaching " of Jesus) can be treated as the subject of a strictly " scientific " investigation. The question whether the miracles really happened is not within the competence of the historian to decide, if we mean by an " historian " someone who approaches the subject with an " open mind " and without preconceived ideas—for the sufficient reason that it is impossible to approach the Gospel records in this way. There is no such thing as an " impartial " historian in this sense : everyone who comes to the Gospels is already either a believer or an unbeliever. The multitudes, according to the Gospel accounts, witnessed the miracles of Jesus as " signs and wonders " ; they came and went away with an " open mind," but they were not edified ; seeing, they had seen and not perceived. Only those who came in faith understood the meaning of the acts of power. That is why any discussion of the Gospel miracles must begin, as we began, with a consideration of the biblical theology, with the faith which illuminates their character and purpose.

Thus, the answer to the question, Did the miracles happen ? is always a *personal* answer. It is not the judgment of an historian *qua* scientific investigator, or the verdict of a school of theologians, or the pronouncement of an authoritative council of churchmen. It is the " Yes " of faith to the challenge which confronts us in the New Testament presentation of Christ —the only Christ we can know. When we say " Yes " to the question about Christ, we are assenting to the apostolic claim that in Him the power of God, which was from the beginning, was made manifest and was active for our salvation " under Pontius Pilate." The present writer can do no more than testify to his conviction that in Christ the power of God was indeed revealed : the miracles *did* happen.

But there are still difficulties in the way of accepting this simple answer. The first is that, if the whole matter may thus be reduced to a single and simple act of faith, might we not have short-circuited the whole discussion of the previous chapters and simply written " I believe " and left the matter there ? The answer to this question is surely that the act of faith, though simple and unambiguous, is nevertheless the act of the whole personality, including the assent of our mind, as well as of our heart and will. In order to make an intelligent assent to the claim of the earliest preachers, it was necessary to know what that claim really was. It was necessary to discover what the earliest makers of the Gospel tradition were trying to say to us when they preserved for us the miracle-stories. When we have to the best of our poor ability honestly made the effort to understand the preaching of the miracle-stories, the assent which we give to the fact of God's act of power in Christ will surely be the richer, the more intelligent and the more sincere.

A second difficulty may appear to be that this kind of an answer—the simple " Yes " of faith—may conceal an over-simplification of the real problem. We may agree in general that Christ had the power of God to work miracles ; but this admission still leaves us with the problem of the historicity of each recorded miracle in the Gospel narratives. Is each recorded miracle-story to be accepted " by faith " on its face value ? Certainly not : we must exercise our critical and historical faculties in respect of the detail of each particular miracle-story. Each must be considered in the light of all the available knowledge which we can bring to bear upon it. The acknowledgment that the power of God was with Jesus in His mighty works is in no sense inconsistent with the admission that our knowledge of His individual acts of power has been mediated to us by a long process of the passing of the tradition from mouth to mouth, from community to community, before it came to be written down. In this process we can trace the motives guiding the development of the tradition in this or that direction ; we can perhaps account for the addition of a phrase here or a detail there, in such a way that, though we are less sure about the exact details of what originally happened, we are more than ever sure that we are in close touch with the mind and purpose—the living faith—of the men who first loved to tell the story. It may be true that we cannot state precisely what happened when Jesus encountered a hungry multitude by the lakeside or a demented outcast amongst the tombs, yet there is still a *residuum* which faith can and must affirm, that the power of God was there made manifest to those who witnessed the act of the Lord, after their eyes had been opened. This is that element of the tradition which only faith can perceive, even if it cannot formulate it ; it is that something which the Gospel-writers have communicated to us " from faith to faith." Perhaps we might say that it is by faith that we know that Jesus worked the mighty works of the power of God ; but, having reached this point through the grace of God, it is by the exercise of our critical intelligence and our historical imagination that we try to determine the nature and circumstances of these works in their historical setting and in the implications which they were perceived to involve for the faith of the earliest Christian disciples.

Thus, we must affirm both the value and the limits of the historical criticism of the Gospels. It is valuable in respect of the light which it can throw upon the making and meaning of the miracle-story tradition in the Gospels ; but it is limited in that it cannot of itself decide for us whether the miracles occurred at all, or if so, which and how. At most it cannot do more than convince us that the associates of Jesus, who stood nearest to Him in time and place, were most assuredly persuaded of His power to work miracles, whereas, on the other hand, for example, they did not believe that John the Baptist worked miracles (cf. John x. 41). It is not possible to state more than that Jesus was believed by those who knew Him best to have worked the very miracles which the prophets had associated with the dawning of the Messianic Age. Faith itself will wish to draw the discreet veil of a reverent agnosticism over the desire to dogmatize as to what was or was not possible, or what precisely happened on any specific occasion ; faith alone can overcome the desire to find " proofs " or to seek for a sign. Each reader of the Gospels must, on the basis of his own studies and insights, make his own estimate of the historical probability of any particular episode for himself.[1] He will not wish to press his own conclusions upon others.

---

[1] Cf. Rawlinson, *St. Mark*, p. 60 : " The broad truth of the Christian doctrine of the Incarnation once assumed, no wise person will proceed rashly to draw the limits between what is and what is not possible ; in particular instances it must be left to the individual reader of the Gospel to judge of the historical probabilities for himself. The truth of Christianity in any case does not stand or fall with the historical accuracy in detail of the miracle-stories in the Gospels."

2. *The Miracle-Stories and the Truth of History*

There is still one point of the greatest importance which remains to be noticed concerning the bearing of the miracle-stories upon the question of history. Even if we admit, having regard to the manner in which the tradition of the Lord's miracles was handed down in the Church, that the precise details of *how* any particular miracle exactly took place cannot be ascertained with certainty by us, there is still an important sense in which the miracle-stories contain the truth of history. That is to say, the issues which were raised by the claim of Jesus to work miracles were the actual " historical " issues which were at stake between Jesus and His disciples on the one hand, and the Pharisees and the multitudes on the other. They concerned the very claims which Jesus made upon His contemporaries, upon disciple and Pharisee, upon friend and foe, upon believer and sceptic and indifferent alike. The course of the discussion of the previous chapters has led us to affirm that Jesus Himself, in His own person, during His own life and ministry, confronted the men and women He encountered with the challenge which was involved in His acts of power. It was not merely that He compelled men to acknowledge that He possessed the power to make a lame man walk : He was not concerned to impress His contemporaries with His marvellous power ; but rather that He asked them by the same token to believe that He had authority upon earth to forgive sins. He not merely opened the eyes of blind men, but claimed by that sign the power to make men see the truth of God. He not merely healed the lepers, the diseased and

the impotent, but demonstrated thereby His ability
to break the power of sin and to enable men to fulfil
the works of the Law. He not merely cast out
dæmons, but saw in His victory over them the
earnest of His triumph over the powers of evil, the
binding of the Strong Man. He not merely fed
hungry men in the desert, but claimed by that sign
to be the dispenser of the spiritual food by which
men's souls are nourished upon their pilgrimage
through a barren land. He not merely commanded
the storm and trod upon the waves of the sea, but
wished His disciples to see thereby in Him the
restrainer alike of the forces of nature and of the madness of the people. And, finally, He not merely
raised a child or a man from the dead, but claimed
in doing so to be the resurrection and the life. It is
the witness of the New Testament, in whole as well
as in part, in St. Mark's Gospel as well as in St.
John's, that Jesus Himself, consciously and deliberately made these claims—although it is implied that
their full significance was not truly appreciated even
by the disciples whom He had chosen to be with
Him until God had set the seal of the divine testimony
upon all His signs by the raising of His Son from the
dead. In the last resort it was the sign of the resurrection which authenticated all Jesus's other signs
and the claims which they involved : " What sign
shewest Thou unto us, seeing that Thou doest these
things ? . . . Destroy this temple, and in three days
I will raise it up . . . When therefore He was raised
from the dead, His disciples remembered that He
spake this ; and they believed the Scripture, and the
word which Jesus had said " (John ii. 18–22).

Although it is doubtless true that even the disciples

did not realize the full implications of the miracles of Jesus until after His resurrection, it is nonetheless true that the issues which underlie the miracle-stories were the living issues with which Jesus confronted His contemporaries through the performance of His mighty works. The Q story of the question of John the Baptist (Matt. xi. 2-6, Luke vii. 18-23) affirms that Jesus Himself saw in His own mighty works the great Christological issue which challenged the unbelief oı His own generation : " Blessed is he who shall find no occasion of stumbling in me." St. Mark in such a story as that of the Healing of the Paralytic (ii. 1-12), no less than St. John in his story of the Man Born Blind (ix. 1 ff.), implies that the miraculous activity of Jesus raised those very questions of the mystery oı His person and His authority to forgive sins, which became in later years the focus of the unresolved controversy between Church and Synagogue, betweeu believer and unbeliever. In many other stories, such as the Beelzebub Controversy or the Sabbath Healings, it is insisted that these Christological issues were the very points of conflict between faith and unbelieı during the ministry of Jesus Himself. They were not issues which were only subsequently perceived and imported into the story of Jesus's life, as it was told at a later period, when the interest of the Church had passed to theology and doctrinal speculation, or which were only later forced to the fore during the controversy with Judaism. On the contrary, these were the living issues with which Jesus actually confronted the men of His time : His authority to bring to men the forgiveness of God, His power to release men from their bondage to sin and the devil, His ability to give them the new life, which was not subïect to the vicissitudes of history or terminable by the limitations of our mortality : in a word, His fulfilment of the ancient promises of God. This is the truth of history which the miracle-stories contain. The miracles of the Gospels are in this sense the witnesses to the truth that in Jesus God's salvation drew nigh to the world of men. This salvation is no mere pious hope, no theological construction of a heaven-aspiring Church, but a reality grounded in concrete events, when the Word was made flesh.

The Gospels show clearly that it was this very offer of salvation, this claim of Jesus to be the fulfilment of Israel's hope, that resulted in the growing hostility of the Jewish religious leaders and finally in their rejection and crucifixion of the Christ of God. It was not that they had not recognized the signs which Jesus wrought ; on the contrary, they had understood them very well—but not by faith. It was not that they merely disagreed with His teaching ; if Jesus had been content merely to teach, it would scarcely have been necessary to put Him to death, since the realistic rulers of the Sanhedrin knew well enough the impotence of ideas and ideals, of ethical precepts and moral appeals. They would not have been afraid of those. It was rather because Jesus gave effect to His teaching in action, not by seizing the sword but by wielding the power of God, that He must be destroyed. It is St. John who brings out this point quite forcibly ; after he has recounted the story of the Raising of Lazarus, he goes on at once to describe how the Jewish rulers immediately decided that Jesus must be put to death :

" Many therefore of the Jews, which came to Mary and beheld that which He did, believed on Him. But some of them went away to the Pharisees, and told them the things which Jesus had done. The chief priests therefore and the Pharisees gathered a council and said, What do we ? for this man doeth many signs. If we let Him thus alone, all men will believe on Him. . . . So from that day forth they took counsel that they might put him to death " (John xi. 45–48a, 53).

The Lazarus story puts into dramatic form the truth of history, whatever may be our view as to whether Jesus did or did not raise a man called Lazarus at Bethany before Passion Week. It was because Jesus by His signs had demonstrated that He was the resurrection and the life, the fulfilment of Judaism and the hope of the world, that He was put to death. This was the actual issue upon which Jesus was crucified ; it was no mere later theological invention of a creed-building Church. Jesus was not crucified because he taught an ethic of love. Apart from the miracles of Jesus, the story of the crucifixion as a historical narrative is unintelligible, and the religious significance of man's rejection of God's demonstrated salvation becomes an anæmic moralism. The miracles of the Gospel are not the figments of a legend-loving Christian community ; they are the hard facts which underline man's rejection of God's salvation and which bring history to a climax and the purpose of God to its fulfilment.

3. *The Religious Value of the Miracle-Stories for Us*

Miracle thus forms a part of the Gospel itself, and it cannot be eliminated from the *history* of the Gospel record. The Gospels assert that in Jesus of Nazareth the eschatological expectation of the prophets of Israel was fulfilled, and there is hardly a miracle-story which does not point to this fulfilment and in which there is not something to correspond to the Scriptural prophecy or the traditional apocalyptic imagery.[1] But the life of Jesus was itself an apocalypse, an unveiling of the truth of God, to those who had eyes to see. To the latter, the miracles of the Gospels were the visible signs that Christ was the realization of the hope of Israel ; they were not a detachable portion of the preaching of the Kingdom of God but a *sine qua non* of it. To those who believe that the power and the purpose of God were manifested in Christ, the miracle-stories are full of instruction, and they were written, like all the Scriptures, for our learning. They are full of direction concerning our attitude and behaviour in the presence of the Lord of Power. Not only do they assure us of the breaking-in of the " last things " upon the plane of world-events, and thus belong to the sphere of the κήρυγμα ; they contain much that is relevant to the conduct of our lives as Christian disciples in the matter of faith and prayer and obedience, and thus they belong to the sphere of διδαχή as well. Moreover, they have long been used as themes of meditation in the realm of both public and private devotion and worship, and much might be written upon the devotional use of the miracle-stories in the history of Christian worship. They speak to us of the gracious dealings of Christ with our sick and hungry and tormented souls, and the ancient power of Christ which they reveal is found by faith to be available still to those who but touch the hem of His garment. They are for the Christian no dead

[1] Cf. an instructive article by Prof. C. H. Dodd in the *Expository Times*, vol. xliv. No. 11 (Aug. 1933), p. 505.

records of wonders of an age that is past and tales of long ago, but parables of the dealings of the living Christ with those who trust Him and obey His Word. They breathe the atmosphere of discipleship and speak the language of devotion : " Lord, I believe : help Thou mine unbelief ! " " Lord, that I may receive my sight ! " " He followed Him in the way." " She arose and ministered unto them."

Therefore, to understand the meaning of the miracle-stories of the Gospel tradition it is first necessary to have penetrated the incognito of Jesus, and to have seen behind the Jesus of Galilee the Christ of New Testament faith. Apart from this faith, the miracles of Jesus, even though our intellects were convinced on " scientific " grounds that they had taken place, could have no more meaning for us than they had for those in the multitude who stood by and were amazed ; they could have no more *saving* significance than the wonderful therapeutic achievements of modern medicine and psychology. They might compel our admiration or evoke our amazement, but Christ does not ask for our admiration but for our faith ; He does not seek to amaze us, but to lead us to call Him by His proper name. We stand entirely outside the New Testament edifice of faith and worship, if we assume that the miracles of Jesus are to be placed in the same category as the successes of modern psycho-therapy, as merely illustrating the general truth of the supremacy of mind over matter or any other modern theory. It is only those to whom it is given to know the mystery of the Kingdom of God who can understand the true significance of the miracles of the Gospel as the acts of the Christ of power. Only when we put aside our theories and rationalizations and accept the witness of the Scriptures can we understand the motives of those who first formulated and handed on the miracle-stories and the purpose of the Evangelists who wrote them down in their Gospels. Then we perceive that it is true of the miracle-stories, as of every other part of the Gospel record, that " these things were written that ye might believe that Jesus is the Christ, the Son of God, and that believing ye might have life in His name " (John xx. 31).

INDEX OF PROPER NAMES

INDEX OF SCRIPTURE REFERENCES

OLD TESTAMENT

THE MIRACLE-STORIES OF THE GOSPELS

LUKE—continued				iv. 53				118
xvii. 5			111 n.	v. 1–18				77
11–19		110, 112		2–9			115, 119
xviii. 1–5			80	8			119 n.
6			111 n.	10, 16–18			119
43			108 n.	17			54 n.
xix. 8			111 n.	19			16
xxi. 27			9	19–47			119
xxii. 31			111 n.	27			119
32			106	39 f.		56 n., 81
51			110 n.	vi. 1–21			106
53			7	2			114
61			111 n.	4		96, 118
69			5 f.	4–13			115
xxiii. 34			57	9			95
xxiv. 3			111 n.	14		95, 113 n.
25–27			82	16–21			115
27			81	17			118
28			93 n.	19			116 n.
30 f.			84 n.	22 ff.			118
35			94	26		14, 115
42 f.			96	30–65			48
				31–33, 49 f., 58		95 f.
JOHN				51–59			96
i. 3			54 n.	vii. 17			121
10			14	20			71 n.
12			7	23			77
14			10, 14 f.	31			114
29, 34, 41			13	viii. 48 f.			71 n.
44			86	27–30			86
48			56	ix. 1–41	13, 77, 115, 117,
ii. 1–11		115, 120			119, 133
6, 9			121	3		31, 60, 62
11			10, 14	5 f.			84 n.
13–22		117, 121	14 ff.			119
18–22		48, 132	16, 33		65, 114
23			114	22			119
iii. 1–21		117, 121	x. 18			7
2			114	20			71 n.
iv. 46–54		78, 115, 118	25, 37 f.			29
48			114, 118	41			130